Distinctively Christian

A Christ-centered Approach to Early Childhood Spiritual Development

Milton V. Uecker, Ed.D.

**Distinctively Christian;
A Christ-centered Approach to Early Spiritual Development**

© 2019 by Dr. Milton V. Uecker

Published by Wheaton Press

Wheaton, Illinois

www.WheatonPress.com

ISBN-10: 1950258009
ISBN-13: 978-1950258000 (WheatonPress.com)

1. Early Childhood Education 2. Education – Teaching. 3. Christian Education. 4. Education – Philosophy. 5. Education & Reference.

Copyright and Trademark Standard

Go to www.WheatonPress.com to learn about additional resources.

WHAT PEOPLE ARE SAYING ABOUT
DISTINCTIVELY CHRISTIAN
A CHRIST-CENTERED APPROACH TO EARLY CHILDHOOD SPIRITUAL DEVELOPMENT

"Long recognized as the 'go to' expert on child development, the truths contained in these pages are relevant in ways that will bring transcendent Truth to early childhood learning."

Todd R. Marrah, Ph.D., Head of School, Tree of Life Christian School

"Distinctively Christian takes deep concepts and puts them into words and phrases that are easily understood and grasped. Outstanding! It makes me teary to see so much of Dr. Milt's life work and philosophy laid out and made so accessible. Every early education program needs this!"

D'Arcy Maher, M.Ed.,
Former Editor for Christian Early Education Magazine,
Former ACSI Director of Early Education Services

"Each chapter includes pertinent Scripture, creative tips, relevant resources and reflective questions, skillfully interwoven with Christian Truth and invaluable insights from Dr. Uecker's lifetime of teaching!"

Jenni Bacon Miller, Director, School Ministries Ohio

"Excellent resource! As a grandparent of nine grandchildren, I want to get this book into the hands of each of my daughters, so they may better understand the elements, process, and stages of spiritual formation in the lives of those we've been entrusted to raise. Every educator as well as parent should read this book!"

Jeffrey Mattner, Ed.D., Regional Director I ACSI Mid-America Region

"Dr. Uecker not only uses his many years of teaching experience and research to explain child development theory and developmental stages, but he infuses his own "God story" in a way that lends authenticity and wisdom along with expertise to this work. Whether you are an administrator or teacher in an early childhood program or a parent seeking to ensure developmental spiritual growth in your young child, you will find this book a treasure. It will quickly become dog-eared as you refer to it as your guide for developing a distinctively Christ-centered early childhood program."

Stacia Emerson, PhD., Associate Professor, Southern Wesleyan University

"Truly the most significant and comprehensive work that I have read describing the components of a truly distinctive Christian early education program! A must-read for early educators in the Christian school movement! This will quickly become the constant companion of early education leaders, teachers, parents, and children's pastors who are serious about laying the foundation for a Christ-centered education and worldview."

Sara Jo Dillard,
Director of Early Education Resources at Association of Christian Schools International., 2002 Recipient of the Roy W. Lowrie Jr. Leadership Award

Contents

Acknowledgements

The early childhood faculty and Dr. Sandi Jolly, program director, at Westminster Catawba Christian School in Rock Hill, South Carolina and D'Arcy Maher for reading a draft of this book and providing their insights and additional resources.

Sara Jo Dillard, ACSI Director of Early Education Resources, , for providing countless opportunities to speak into the lives of early childhood educators and persistently encouraging me to write this book.

Dr. Connie Mitchell, Dean of the College of Education at Columbia International University, for her collaboration in designing the model for a curriculum framework and the professional development seminars that followed.

Christa Anderson Dysart, for allowing me to adapt her Bible timeline narrative, written for the upper elementary level, for use at the early childhood level

Preface

One of my early education heroes was Mr. Fred Rogers. I, along with my wife and three boys, visited his neighborhood daily and I was deeply impacted by his knowledge of children, his voice, his gentleness, and his lifelong dedication to what for him was a clear calling to minister grace and love to young children via television.

His attitude of gratitude was clearly reflected in his lifetime achievement award acceptance speech at the Daytime Emmy Awards ceremony in 1997. Inspired by his humility, I paraphrase and contextualize his speech:

> *So many people have spoken into my life and contributed to this book, both with and without their knowledge. It is with a deep sense of gratitude for their role in shaping my philosophy and calling as a Christian early childhood educator, that I dedicate this book to them. Some of them are reading this book, some may never read it, and some are now in heaven.*
>
> *These individuals have loved me and shared life with me. Some were teachers, colleagues, and mentors, and others have been on the sidelines cheering me on. I now pause to think of them and thank God for them.*
>
> *Perhaps you too can pause and give thanks for the people that God has used in your life to shape you as His follower and servant.*

I thank God for His enduring love and as I remember how He has used:

My wife, Linda, who has exemplified so much of what is shared within the pages of this book. She, apart from Jesus, is God's greatest gift to me, and it is her love for Jesus, for me, and for our children that shaped and supported my walk and vocation.

My sons, Joel, Josh, and Jeremy, who were a *"lab"* of sorts, and who now exemplify the validity of the ideas and principles within this book as they love their wives and raise my nine grandchildren to love and follow Christ.

Dr. Gene Garrick, who instilled in me a love for Christian school philosophy.

Dr. Roy W.Lowrie Jr. and his wife Margaret, who encouraged me to earn my doctorate, challenged me to envision myself as an advocate for Christian early education, and who launched my role in higher education.

My former colleagues at Norfolk Christian School, Jeanette Hilton, Barbara Thierry, Linda McIntire, Susie Prevette, Avie Carlisle and Cindy Megginson for modeling a developmental philosophy of Christian education,

The College of Education faculty members at Columbia International University for the hours that we spent around the lunch table discussing ways in which to better prepare teachers for their roles within Christian Schools.

Introduction: The Need for a Distinctively Christian Early Education Program

My introduction to early childhood education would be considered by many a coincidence. But my viewpoint, in light of my worldview, is that God not only called me to be a Christian school educator, but that He opened an unexpected doorway to a more specific purpose---that of understanding and instructing the young child.

In the spring of 1972 I found myself in need of a recertification course. I was teaching second grade in Texas and I had an opportunity to take a course in early childhood curriculum at a nearby elementary school. Since the course was offered at a convenient time and place, I enrolled. Within weeks the enthusiasm and passion of Dr. Alberta Castenada, a professor at the University of Texas, captured not only my interest, but my heart.

My subsequent M.Ed. in Curriculum and Instruction at the University of. Texas in Austin included as many courses in early education as was possible. Equipped with a developmentally appropriate philosophy, I set out to focus this newly acquired philosophy within the context of the rapidly emerging Christian school movement. In 1975 God led me to Norfolk Christian School in Norfolk, Virginia. I did not know it at the time, but their early education program, grounded in a developmental approach, was a rare find.

Through exposure to other Christian school programs, I learned that there was a tension between my "progressive" philosophy and a more traditional curriculum-centered approach that was the dominant practice within Christian schools. The belief that developmentally appropriate practices were humanistic and incompatible with a Christian philosophy of education created a dilemma. Was my calling to serve in Christian schools in conflict with my philosophy of early education? God, through the leading of the Holy Spirit, introduced me to like-minded educators who could answer my questions and resolve my doubts.

In the summer of 1976 Norfolk Christian sent me to my first International Institute for Christian School Teachers at Grace College in Winona Lake, Indiana. This Institute provided an opportunity for Christian school educators to gather from across the country and be trained in a Christian philosophy of education. It was here that I was first exposed to a biblical or Christian approach to curriculum and instruction. Four women were used by God to not only encourage me, but through their teaching, began laying the foundation for my role as a Christian educator.

Eunice Dirks and Peg Lowrie stressed, with reference to biblical truth, the need for understanding children and building early education curriculum around their unique way of thinking and learning. Ruth Haycock demonstrated how throughout her devotional life she noted any and all scripture related to teaching, learning, and curricular disciplines. She challenged each of us to do the same. Martha MacCullough's teaching examined what has come to be known as research-based "best practices" and then verified, corrected or expanded the ideas through the integration of God's word. I left the Institute having taken the first steps in developing what J.P. Moreland refers to as the ability to view one's vocational calling through the lens of a biblical worldview.[1]

I also recall another pivotal lecture that occurred in my first doctoral class at the University of Virginia. The class was a foundations of curriculum course. It seemed the logical place to begin in light of my pursuit of another degree in Curriculum and Instruction with Early Childhood as its focal point. The class was discussing the first chapter of Curriculum: Principles and Practices.[2] The discussion centered upon the necessity to develop curriculum with a specific and consistent focus on a philosophical position (what is today commonly referred to as worldview). Zais summarized the options as the choice between nature, man, or the transcendent (other-worldly / a god). The resulting worldview was to serve as the focal point for everything done within a school program. Curriculum is grounded in a coherence factor or, as referred to by Neil Postman, one of the "gods" of past and present education.[3]

The point was made that it is was not the role of the university to insist upon a specific worldview, but to encourage educators to develop curriculum from the perspective of their worldview's narrative. It was that statement that became the basis for examining everything through the lens of scripture with Christ as the coherence factor. The result was that I graduated with a *"Christian"* education forged through the habit of thinking Christianly about every aspect of child development and early education.

It has been this "habit", to think Christianly about education, that I have sought to model during my subsequent twenty-seven years as a professor of early childhood at both Regent and Columbia International Universities, and it is likewise the motivation for this book. Experience has shown me that teachers, being pragmatic in their orientation, attend to what they do, as opposed to the philosophical basis for their beliefs and instructional choices.

As a result, programs and teachers can become so focused on reading and writing that they neglect what it means to be thoroughly Christian.

The inverse is also possible when the faith-based elements so dominate the program that it resembles a five-day Sunday school.

Christian early childhood programs must be both distinctively Christian and thoroughly academic. They have the responsibility to lay the foundation for spiritual growth and provide the knowledge, skills and dispositions that are the groundwork for academic success. Erring in one direction at the cost of the other occurs when biblical truth is an add-on (value-added) as opposed to being integrated into every aspect the of the school's purpose and practices---mission, vision, outcomes, instruction and curriculum.

> **PROGRAMS AND TEACHERS MUST BE ABLE TO NOT ONLY MAKE STATEMENTS ABOUT TEACHING FROM A BIBLICAL WORLDVIEW, BUT UNDERSTAND THE IMPACT OF A BIBLICAL WORLDVIEW ON ALL THAT IS SAID AND DONE WITHIN THE CLASSROOM.**

The pages that follow will address the primary distinctive of Christian early education. All early education programs educate, and they all transform, but the nature of the transformation varies in accordance with the school's beliefs related to God, truth, value and humankind (men, women, boys and girls). The apostle Paul devoted all his energy to presenting every man complete in Christ (Col. 1:26). In like manner, Christian early education exists to lay the foundation for a life in Christ and encourage "first steps" in the process referred to as spiritual formation.

Readers will think through the distinctive mission and vision of Christian early education and the means by which outcomes related to the spiritual formation of the young child can be realized. It is my desire to not just communicate with those serving in Christian schools but with all who are committed to nurturing and teaching young children within the home, church, daycare, Bible clubs, and released time and after school programs. Hopefully the insights and practices can likewise lay a foundation for college students as they prepare to teach within Christian early childhood classrooms.

Chapter One: Bringing Clarity to a Program's Mission, Vision and Desired Outcomes

What we have heard and learned—

that which our ancestors have told us—

4 we will not hide from their descendants.

We will tell the next generation

about the LORD's praiseworthy acts,

about his strength and the amazing things he has done.

5 He established a rule in Jacob;

he set up a law in Israel.

He commanded our ancestors

to make his deeds known to their descendants,

6 so that the next generation, children yet to be born,

might know about them.

They will grow up and tell their descendants about them.

7 Then they will place their confidence in God.

They will not forget the works of God,

and they will obey his commands.

Psalm 78: 3-7 (NET)

God's word is the revelation of God, His thoughts, desires, and purposes. It is His voice assuring us of His love and will for us. It is His desire that every man, woman and child be redeemed in Christ, transformed, and then sent on mission. His general calling as seen in Matthew 28:18-29 (referred to as the Great Commission) is general in the sense that it is the task given every believer. We have also been given gifts (1 Cor. 1:4-11) and abilities that are tailored for a specific vocational calling, a calling which often includes a heart for a specific place or people group. Many of you, like me, have been called to teach and disciple within the context of a Christian school and more specifically placed into classrooms or programs where young children are the "people group".

WE ARE ON A MISSION.

> WE ARE TELLING THE "NEXT GENERATION ABOUT THE LORD'S PRAISEWORTHY ACTS, AND ABOUT HIS STRENGTH, AND THE AMAZING THINGS HE HAS DONE."

WE SHARE A VISION.

> A DREAM WHEREIN THE NEXT GENERATION PLACES ITS CONFIDENCE IN GOD, DOES NOT FORGET GOD'S WORKS, OBEYS HIM, AND THEN IN TURN GROWS UP TESTIFYING OF THEIR FAITH IN HIM TO THE NEXT GENERATION.

Christ-centered early education programs are established to focus their attention not only on a child's cognitive, social and physical readiness, the purpose of all preschools and kindergartens, but to also direct their attention to the whole child which includes the faith or spiritual development of the child (Luke 2:52).

The purpose of the school or early education program clarifies what the program will do. It is the mission, however, that defines what the educational activities within the school will accomplish.

The mission and vision are the starting point for curriculum because it is when we begin with the end in mind that we define and clarify our desired outcomes and end results.

It is the "billboard" that portrays the distinctives of its product or what a child at the end (prior to moving to the next level of their schooling) will know, be able to do, value and believe.

Too often an early education program either has no mission or vision, or, when part of a preschool through grade twelve program, only identifies with the broader mission of the school. The problem with the latter is that there is no provision for the specific preschool and kindergarten outcomes needed to guide its practices and validate the program.

The Curriculum Framework[4]

Essential Beliefs

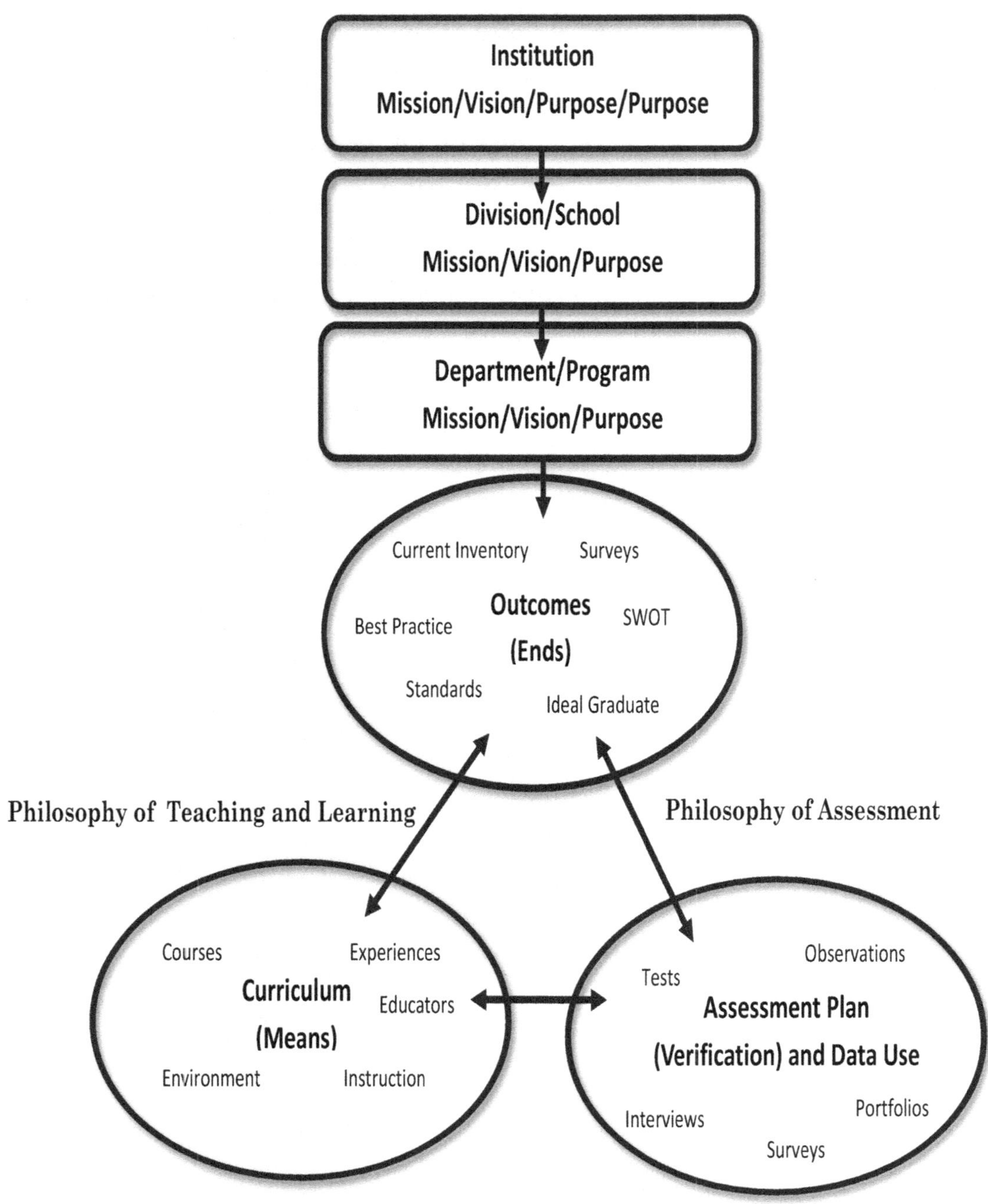

The mission and vision are the opening elements of the framework. The Christian early education framework, in addition to its cognitive, social and physical expectations, because of its distinct nature, must articulate an intention to impact the child's spiritual development. The vision must subsequently define what is meant by spiritual formation during early childhood through its articulation of the spiritual expectations.

Since the framework's purpose, mission, and vision are often found in brochures, parent handbooks, and online, the fulfillment of these intentions is directly related to the integrity of the program. Families are trusting the school to not only engage in its purpose but also accomplish its mission. All content and instructional activities within the school can and should be consistently linked to its intended outcomes.

The labels for each part of a framework are secondary to their function, therefore, attention should be given to the purpose of each element. In the end it is the content, regardless of its label, that is critical. Some schools, for example, may call the vision the "portrait of a program completer or graduate".

The Purpose

Many programs do not have a purpose statement separate from a mission statement. In fact, many view the two as being synonymous. A curriculum framework, as illustrated in the graphic, need not have a purpose statement because it does not imply specific outcomes. An explanation of the purpose statement is helpful, however, in evaluating one's current mission statement.

A purpose statement contains phrases like:

- The program partners with parents…
- The ABC Preschool supports the home in its effort to "train up a child in the way he should go".

- Through a Christ-centered philosophy and biblical worldview teachers strive to provide a successful first step in a child's education.
- Teachers model Christ and create classroom learning communities where children are nurtured and encouraged.

These examples all have purpose in common. They state what classrooms will be like and what teachers will do.

What they fail to do is point out the end result of what is done.

In the past there was an assumption that if one did all these things that the child would learn or grow spiritually. Even if this were true, without an idea of specific or intended outcomes, how is one to know the effectiveness of the program? The following is an example of a purpose statement where the focus is on what the program does:

> *The ABC preschool supports XYZ church, its parents and the surrounding community by providing a biblically-based preschool where children can learn within an atmosphere of love and age-appropriate learning activities.*

If you discover that your program actually has a purpose, as opposed to a mission statement, label it as such or amend the purpose statement by adding the desired outcomes. Label the combination of purpose and outcomes as the mission. There is also the option of keeping the purpose statement and writing a separate mission statement.

The Mission

The mission statement makes the primary goals of the program clear. It provides categories or "files" wherein all outcomes can be organized. It gives direction to its activities and provides the criteria needed to verify whether-or not the program is doing what it has set out to do.

This mission statement example provides seven areas of focus.

It is the mission of ABC 's preschool-kindergarten unit to instill within each student a love of learning, and the academic, physical, social and spiritual foundations needed for success as children enter first grade. It also strives to develop a partnership with families that results in effective parenting skills and school involvement that supports the child's emotional and spiritual growth and academic success.[5]

Everything the school hopes to accomplish must fit within these categories:

- **Students**Students
  - Love of learning
  - Academic foundations
  - Physical foundations
  - Social foundations
  - Spiritual foundations

Parents

  - Effective parenting skills
  - School involvement

At this point the framework provides an initial understanding of what a program will strive to accomplish but one does not yet understand what is meant by each of these categories.

  - What does love of learning look like?
  - What are the academic, physical, social and spiritual foundations needed for success as they enter first grade?
  - What does the program mean by effective parenting skills and what behaviors define the involved parent?

The Vision

The vision is the amplified version of the mission.

Think in terms of an address to perspective parents in which each of the mission's files are opened and explained (one paragraph per file). The impact or end results of the early education program are clarified. In order to provide the content, the program's teachers and other stakeholders should brainstorm and research the knowledge, skills and dispositions related to each of the ends (or files) within the mission. The resulting list is then shortened by eliminating or combining similar ideas and then prioritizing the remaining expectations.

In keeping with the inclusion of spiritual foundations as a priority within a Christian early ed program, this spiritual dimension will serve as an example. The process might begin with a review of desired outcomes within professional literature related to the spiritual formation of young children. Through reflection and discussion, administration and faculty can use the information, along with their own brainstorming, to create a list of desired outcomes for the culminating level of the program (preschool or kindergarten). Additional outcomes, in keeping with the values of the church or school, can also be added. The list below serves as an example.

Knowledge:

Students will come to *know* that...

- God created the heavens and the earth
- God is all powerful and knows all things
- God is always present, and He cares for us
- God is our Father, Jesus is God's Son; the Holy Spirit is our helper (the Trinity)
- The Bible is God's book and it is true
- The Bible contains God's story (redemptive plan)
- The Bible shows us what kind of people we should be

- God's commands, which tell us what is right and wrong, are found in the Bible
- All people are made in God's image and are unique and wonderfully made
- All people are sinners and need a Savior because they have disobeyed God
- When Jesus died on the cross it was for all people, to take the punishment and provide forgiveness for their sins
- Jesus has prepared a place in heaven for those who follow Him

Skills:

Students are able to....

- Memorize and recite Bible verses
- Offer praise and worship
- Pray

Dispositions: *(values, beliefs, attitudes)*

Students desire or choose to...

- Confess sins and ask Jesus to be their Saviour
- Talk to God through prayer
- Love him, follow him, and bring Him Glory
- Choose to honour and obey God and parents
- Worship God
- Attend to God's word and share it with others
- Love, respect, be thankful and serve others

The vision need not include every potential outcome but capture the essence of the mission through including the areas of priority. The result should, however, reflect key aspects of a biblical worldview by including areas related to God, truth, man and biblical values. There can be additional instructional outcomes, but those within the vision are the primary public goals and subject to annual assessment.

An example of the Spiritual Foundations component within the vision:

Spiritually children will come to know that there is one true God, the creator of heaven and earth, who loves and cares for them. The Bible will be viewed as God's words to us, totally true and absolutely reliable. They will come to know God's redemptive plan as revealed through the Bible's narrative, and understand that he or she is a sinner, who can be cleansed or forgiven by God through Jesus's death on the cross. They learn to pray as a means of communication with God. Children will have respect for and submission to parents and teachers by consistently choosing cheerful, complete, and immediate obedience. Love for others will be evident as they seek to serve, share and cooperate with one another. They will view themselves as individuals uniquely created by God with gifts and talents to be used for His glory.[6]

The Outcomes (restatement of the vision as outcomes)

This phase of the framework development involves the translation of the goals within the vision into outcome statements. The resulting outcomes are sometimes also referred to as goals or standards. The outcomes are made explicit through the restatements. Methods for writing outcome statements vary, but once a style is selected, it should be used consistently. The outcome statements should reflect performances that can be used for assessment.

Examples of Outcomes:

- Children will decide to ask Jesus to be their Savior and to follow Him
- Children will communicate with God beyond the use of memorized prayers by expressing their own thoughts, needs and emotions
- Children will confess specific examples of their sin and ask God for forgiveness

- Children will demonstrate love and care for others by offering to help them and share things that God has provided.
- Children will accept themselves, including their differences, through their expression of thankfulness to God and by their acknowledging that God has given them abilities to be used for his glory.

The Curriculum *(the means to accomplish the outcomes)*

With mission, vision and outcomes in place the platform for curriculum has been prepared. Curriculum is simply all that will be said and done as a means of realizing the outcomes. Curriculum is developed or evaluated through the process of examining each outcome to determine if the means to achieve the outcome are available. A series of questions, like those listed below, should be answered to both clarify and guide in the process.

- What content specific materials, i.e. books and visuals, will be needed to reach this goal?
- What instructional strategies will facilitate the learning?
- What first-hand experiences, i.e. field trips, classroom visitors, should be included?
- How can classroom environment contribute to reaching this outcome?

The answers to these questions are the components of the curriculum, and when available and utilized, they provide the means to accomplishing the mission. The curriculum can then be overviewed through a table that lists the outcomes and the necessary means.

Example of a curriculum matrix:

The Outcome	Materials	Instructional Strategies	Experiences	Classroom Environment
Children will communicate with God beyond the use of memorized prayers	The Bible: Stories related to prayer Children's Literature: What is prayer? [7] The Lord's prayer[8]	Use ACTS acronym, parts of a prayer Incorporating prayer into classroom routine, (individual, in pairs and as a group)	Teacher models' short personal prayers as well as the parts of prayer Sharing answers to prayer	Regular bulletin board displays related to prayer

Assessment

The framework is not complete until an assessment plan has been developed. Given a clearly defined objective, the means whereby the outcome will be verified is reflected by the outcome's verb. The plan can be organized through a second matrix. This matrix will include the objective, the means (implied by the verb) whereby the student demonstrates or makes explicit his or her learning, the person who is responsible to perform the assessment, and the context or timing of the assessment.

Where appropriate, the method of measurement (converting data into numbers) should also be indicated. Performance data related to each outcome should ideally be gathered from students during the weeks or days prior to completing the program. The effectiveness of the curriculum, simply stated, is based upon the percentage of completers who demonstrate the criteria needed to verify a positive performance.

Example of the assessment matrix:

The Outcome	The student will:	Teacher	Context and timing	Measurement
Children will communicate with God beyond the use of memorized prayers	Communicate (pray) simple non-memorized prayers within the classroom and at home	Classroom anecdotal records and a survey question for parents regarding the nature of their child's prayers	Classroom prayer time and final parent conference which includes a question regarding parent observations. An alternative means would be including the question in an online survey	Frequency Evidence that the child is using conversational prayers. Use of rubric to score as yes or no

Living the Curriculum

Share the Mission and Vision with the public. It should be presented within all marketing materials, within the program website, and overviewed during program tours and admission interviews.

Provide the entire framework to perspective teachers prior to and during the interview process.

> **DURING INTERVIEWS ASK QUESTIONS TO DETERMINE THE CANDIDATE'S UNDERSTANDING AND DESIRE TO EMBRACE AND CARRY OUT THE MISSION.**

Select a couple of the outcomes and inquire as to what he or she might do within the classroom to reach these outcomes.

Annually analyze the assessment data to evaluate the effectiveness of the curriculum.

If an objective falls short of expectations, consider changes that might result in more children reaching the goal. Evaluate whether all the components within the curriculum matrix are in place, being utilized, or in need of replacement.

- If needed, select areas of the vision that need revision or change. Justify all changes by focusing on the mission.
- Tie strategic planning and annual budgeting to changes that require funding.

Reflect and Respond

1. What are the enduring ideas (ideas at the heart of the matter and professional competency) found within this chapter?

2. How would you explain the importance of a Christian early education program's mission and vision to a colleague?

3. Based upon the content of this chapter, what are some of the distinctive elements of a Christian early education program?

4. Evaluate your classroom practices and program. To what degree is your instruction contributing to the fulfillment of the school's mission and the mission of Christian early education? Can you identify strengths and weaknesses both as a teacher and within the program as a whole?

5. Identify responses (action points) to what you have learned.

Chapter Two: Faith Development

"Hear, O Israel! The LORD *is our God, the* LORD *is one!* [5] *You shall love the* LORD *your God with all your heart and with all your soul and with all your might.* [6] *These words, which I am commanding you today, shall be on your heart.* [7] *You shall teach them diligently to your sons and shall talk of them when you sit in your house and when you walk by the way and when you lie down and when you rise up.* [8] *You shall bind them as a sign on your hand and they shall be as [b]frontals [c]on your forehead.* [9] *You shall write them on the doorposts of your house and on your gates.*

Deuteronomy 6:4-9

"You will keep this practice forever as a statute for yourselves and your descendants. [25] *Thus, when you have entered the land which the Lord will give you as he promised, you must observe this rite.* [26] *When your children ask you, 'What does this rite of yours mean?'* [27] *you will reply, 'It is the Passover sacrifice for the Lord, who passed over the houses of the Israelites in Egypt; when he struck down the Egyptians, he delivered our houses.'"*

Exodus 12: 24-27a (NIV).

Faith development is directly related to both cognitive and moral development.[9] In each case growth in one area impacts the others. James Fowler has identified six stages in the development of faith, three of which impact the early childhood years. Fowler believes that varying aspects of faith, including a person's relationships with others, view of reality, ways of responding to authority, and cognitive understanding change with time.[10]

When discussing faith', Fowler is not referring to Christian faith or any particular system of belief, but rather, the system of relating to "knowing or construing by which persons apprehend themselves as related to the Transcendent...." (page 5). Fowler views faith as multifaceted. It is composed of one's system of thought or worldview and the ability to take another's perspective.

Faith includes positions on moral issues along with a system for making moral decisions. Understanding what determines the limits to one's 'community of faith', relationship to authority, reasoning strategies, and a response to symbols are also facets of faith.[11] These dimensions, though seemingly complex, are identifiable with aspects of social, cognitive and moral development.

Primal Faith

Fowler identifies the first stage (stage zero) as **primal faith.**[12] This is fundamental to all faith and aligns with Erickson's views on the formation of trust.[13] The Greek word for trust is the idea or word most closely aligned with and translated as faith in English and it is at this time, birth to two, that trust is established through the nurture of and relationship to primary caregivers. Without this foundation the ability to trust is jeopardized in all areas of life. In light of this, it is the nature of the relationship between caregivers and infants that is the foundation for the faith curriculum in infant daycare. Gentle tones of voice, satisfaction of basic needs, and an atmosphere of love, that is identifiable with the name of Jesus, are vital experiences toward faith formation.

Without these experiences later spiritual or faith development is placed at-risk in that trust is essential to starting and maintaining a relationship.

Intuitive-projective Faith

Intuitive-projective faith (stage one), because of its characteristics, can also be referred to as impressionistic faith. The biblical concept of teaching in Deut. 6:4 is related to establishing a deep impression. The impressions would not come through formal teaching, but rather through first hand experiences throughout the day. It is the impact or impressions of these experiences on the mind and emotions that form the "deep and lasting images" or symbols that are the basis of a given faith. Cognitively these might be referred to as the "frames" for one's faith.[14]

Because children are concrete and literal, the faith frames created within a home or classroom are remembered (Proverbs 22:6) and link the security that accompanies a frame with the security found within a relationship with God. Early childhood educators, therefore, need not view ritual as a negative or meaningless exercise. For children, rituals are dynamic experiences. It is through the repeated activities of faith that the abstract becomes real.

It is the activity and experience that causes children to ask faith related questions and develop the understandings that accompany the symbols. This is more clearly illustrated through the celebration of holidays. Holidays are motivational learning tools. A child's attention is given over to each special or "holy" day. Every symbol is a reminder of the day and with each symbol there is a memory and meaning. This grows not only out of the motivation attached to the day, but also to the experiential nature of celebrations.

These celebrations involve all the senses and are repeated throughout the formative years. Even as adults the memories of celebrations remain clear. God designed children and He knows their primary learning style and its relationship to faith formation.

God built upon this when he instructed His people on how to teach. Passover is an example of the use of celebration and its relationship to impressionistic faith. God told His people to establish a Passover celebration as a permanent ordinance and as a memorial "throughout your generations". (Exodus 12:14). Each aspect of the celebration was linked to the story of God's power and faithfulness to His promise to Israel. "And it will come about when your children will say to you, 'What does this rite mean to you?' that you shall say…" (Exodus 13:26).

CELEBRATIONS SET THE STAGE FOR STORY AND STORY INVOLVES BOTH CONCEPT AND EMOTION (THE HEART).

Passover was one of many holy days in the curriculum of the Hebrew nation (e.g. Feast of Weeks, Feast of Booths, Day of Atonement, and Purim). The classroom celebrations of faith and resulting thematic units, when taught consistently, are important to stage one faith. Celebrations should be designed in a way that actively engages students, stimulates their senses, and promotes questioning.

Christmas and Easter should take center stage in that the truths that permeate these times of celebration are so important to the redemptive narrative and faith development. These are also critical within the context of a culture that has secularized these days through the removal of the God story and His glory.

Both Christmas and Easter are preceded by days of preparation (Advent and Lent) which allow for an emphasis over time (four to six weeks). Some of my favorite memories center on these joyous occasions, both during my role as program director at Norfolk Christian and as a father of three sons. I find joy not only in the memories, but also as I observe my own sons passing along some of the traditions formed during early childhood to their sons and daughters.

MEANINGFUL CELEBRATIONS INVOLVE PLANNING AND THE PREPARATION OF THE MEANS WHEREBY THE HOLIDAY BECOMES A "HOLY-DAY".

The focus on Christmas, for example, begins four weeks prior to Christmas as the season of preparation, Advent, is observed.

Within the school context it would begin four weeks prior to Christmas break. The advent wreath with its five candles, four around the wreath and the Jesus or birthday candle in the center, is placed within a prominent position in the chapel or classroom. Each week during chapel an additional candle is lit, and a lesson attached to the candle is emphasized.

The advent theme, as expressed through the candles, should be decided upon prior to advent. For example, candle one represents the fact that His coming was foretold, candle two that his coming was fulfilled, candle three that he wants to come to children as Savior and candle four that He is coming again. In this example the theme centers on "Comings". The candles could also represent important persons within the Christmas narrative--- the Prophets, Mary and Joseph, the Shepherds and the Angels or themes like hope, love, joy and peace.

In each case children are being presented truths related to the Christmas celebration. Throughout advent the children also can be preparing their special birthday present for Jesus. The question is asked, "What would Jesus want?

Ideas related to his heart for the poor, homeless and the lost can be emphasized as fitting gifts. In keeping with these possibilities, an appropriate cause or recipient for the gift can be chosen and revealed to the children---supporting a missionary who serves among a lost people group, purchasing coats for children in need, contributing to a disaster recovery effort, collecting food for a soup kitchen etc.

It is helpful for the children to have a visitor representing the chosen ministry or prepare a powerpoint presentation with pictures that enable the children to "visit" the context in which the gift will be received.

Throughout the four weeks children bring their offerings for the Christmas gift and they begin to get excited as they see the gift growing in size. The time of preparation culminates in the last chapel or "birthday party".

At this chapel, each class shares a specially prepared Christmas song as a praise offering. At the appointed time, with great fanfare, the birthday candle is lit to the reframe of "Happy Birthday" to Jesus. Finally, the birthday gift is presented to a representative of the receiving organization and the total amount of the gift revealed.

EVEN THOUGH NO ONE MAY ASK FOR OR LEAD THE WAY,

CHILDREN SEEM TO NATURALLY CHEER AND BREAK OUT IN APPLAUSE.

The chapel ends with the singing of Joy to the World and a return to their classrooms for a birthday party with games, and of course the birthday cake.

Each year the cake is created through the use of a lamb shaped cake mold so that when the children ask, "Why does the cake look like a lamb?' the opportunity to refer to Jesus as the Lamb of God links truth to the celebration. Even though the youngest children may not fully understand this relationship, the experience will be remembered and in time the understanding will develop.

Like Christmas, Easter is proceeded by six weeks of preparation---the season of lent. During this time the curriculum emphasis should be on the ministry of Jesus. During Bible time and chapels, children can learn or know the heart of Jesus though "observing" what Jesus did.

Just prior to Easter break the children should begin to understand that He came to serve, seek and save the lost. As teachers emphasize the need for a Savior because of sin, the children are led to consider their own sin and need for forgiveness.

With this background the stage is set for a chapel or classroom experience at the end of the day just prior to Easter break.

Teachers assist children in preparing a statement as to why Jesus had to die for them. Four or five-year-old students complete a statement like, "Jesus died for me because…" For children who are two or three the statement might simply be "…because sometimes I disobey".

Each of their responses, written and mounted on black construction paper, is brought to chapel and at an appointed time deposited in a basket at the foot of the cross where a single candle is burning.

ONCE EACH CHILD HAS BROUGHT THEIR NEED TO THE CROSS THE FINAL WORDS OF JESUS, "IT IS FINISHED", ARE ANNOUNCED AND THE CANDLE EXTINGUISHED.

At this point the basket with their statements is carried away in silence and the children's school day ends. Upon their return after Easter they immediately return to a dimly lit quiet chapel setting. The leader announces, as the lights are turned on and the darkness is dispelled, that "He is Risen" to which they respond, "He is Risen indeed." Children then stand and sing "Jesus Christ is Risen Today". While singing, older children come down the aisle carrying Easter lilies and the last person carries the basket where they had previously deposited their words of confession.

As the papers are passed out to each child they note a change. Stamped across the paper in large red letters is the statement, "Paid in Full". Because Jesus died for us and rose again, sins are forgiven once the decision has been made to let Him be the boss and subsequently follow Him. The remainder of the chapel was characterized by songs of joyful praise and upon returning to their classroom they might even experience the only party that is held at the beginning of the day.

A lasting impact is created as cake is served in the morning. This was no ordinary cake, but a lamb cake that was a copy of Jesus' birthday cake, with one important change---the lamb was adorned with a crown.

Again, in keeping with the children of Israel asking why they were eating bitter herbs during the Passover meal, the children may ask (with a bit of encouragement), why the lamb is wearing a crown.

The reason is then the focus of that day's Bible lesson. "Jesus now seated beside God and is King of Kings and Lord of Lords".

These Christmas and Easter celebrations, developed over time, became traditions throughout the program. A holiday curriculum of sorts need not have all of these elements, but regardless of what is done the days should be filled with sensory input, meaningful instruction, worship, joy, and service.

KEEP IN MIND THAT THIS IS THE STAGE OF IMPRESSIONISTIC FAITH--- IMPRESSIONS THAT ARE DEEP AND LASTING AND RECALLED THROUGHOUT A LIFETIME.

Each early childhood program may select additional days to be celebrated. Consider possibilities throughout the calendar along with the truths that might be included during the days leading up to the holiday. Consider days like Veteran's Day, St. Patrick's Day, Mother's and Father's Day, and or other cultural holidays (Romans 14:5-9, Phillips). The world, and media in particular, fill children's minds with images and ideas that are often not biblical and rooted in a secular or materialistic worldview.

Rather than ignoring a "secular" celebration, use the occasion to counter the world's thinking with an enduring biblical truth (see appendix C for suggested themes).

Mythic-literal Faith

Mythic-literal faith (stage two) is also referred to as narrative faith. (Fowler). It is during this time that faith stories are the primary teaching tool. Children during the concrete operations can now begin to see the connections and build the framework for God's redemptive story.

The celebrations in stage one were to be a catalyst for telling the story to the stage two children. God again provides the curriculum through the presentation of His word in story format throughout the Old and New Testaments.

The stories of a faith group create a sense of belonging and community. Parents, grandparents, and teachers also have their own personal faith stories to tell. There are missionary stories in the form of books and story charts and there are testimonies of believers all of which can be presented within the home, school, and church.

These stories are important to the child's emerging sense of selfhood. Stories become part of the child's personal identity and even in cases where opportunities for spiritual development are no longer available, due to a lack of opportunity within a faith context, the truths of childhood are seldom forgotten.

Extending Knowledge and Beliefs into Practice

- Create a classroom community that is not only safe physically but emotionally. Safe classrooms are developmentally appropriate and well managed. They are free of put downs and all bullying. Within this context, talk of Jesus' presence and His care for each of them.
- Offer warm as opposed to cold interactions. Warm interactions offer expressions of love, thankfulness, respect, and joy toward the children. Cold interactions are task oriented and all business. In daycare, for example, the changing of a diaper would be characterized by a gentle touch, soft words of reassurance, and a song being delivered by a smiling face. In contrast cold interactions may involve little more than a quick change and statement like, "be still" or no language interaction at all.
- Decorate the classroom with bulletin boards or murals that visually depict faith and the truths of scripture and intentionally reference the meaning of the images.

Reflect and Respond

1. Think about your student's attitudes. Do behaviors reflect feelings of security, joy, a desire to be there, and confidence during participation in academic and other tasks? What difference does it make?

2. In what ways do classrooms reflect a Christian worldview? What might be done to better communicate truth through the classroom visuals?

3. What messages are the students receiving through your attitudes and body language?

4. Examine the degree to which celebrations are used to communicate truth? How might the curriculum create additional opportunities to build faith-centered memories?

5. Is the classroom designed to respond to biblical teaching with play? Is there a puppet stage and a variety of puppets as a means to reenact a story? Are you observing and listening to play as a means of assessing a child's understanding of lessons? Think through props that can be inserted into the block and home centers to prompt playing about their learning. Collect a variety of cloth remnants (colors, patterns and textures) and cut the pieces into large squares, triangles and circles. The cloth shapes can then be used by the children to create costumes as they reenact the stories.

Chapter Three: Worldview Integration: Reality

All things were created through Him and for Him. And He is before all things, and in Him all things consist.

Colossians 1:16-17

For the LORD is good and his love endures forever; his faithfulness continues through all generations.

Psalm 100:5 (NIV)

For the things that are seen are temporary, but the things that are not seen are eternal.

II Corinthians. 4:18

Even though teaching from the perspective of a biblical or Christian worldview is a phrase used within Christian schools, an understanding of worldview is often lacking. Schooling, through its environment, curriculum and values, develops a worldview regardless of whether or not worldview is one of the intended outcomes. Schools teach, and children come to know the answers to life's important questions and these answers, as a whole, provide the framework or viewpoint through which one's life is governed.

Branson S. Howse defines worldview as

"...THE LENS, GLASSES, FRAMEWORK OR GRID THROUGH WHICH YOU LOOK AT THE WORLD AND EVERY ISSUE OF LIFE...YOUR WORLDVIEW IS THE FOUNDATION OF YOUR IDEAS AND VALUES AND YOUR IDEAS AND VALUES ARE THE FOUNDATION OF YOUR CONDUCT".[15]

Even though worldview deals with philosophy, and the vocabulary and concepts often require higher level thinking, children can develop basic understandings during childhood. A child's moral foundation, according to Barna, is in place by age nine and that worldview is developed between the ages of 18 months and age 13.[16]

Early educators teach worldview through immersion. Everything that is said and done within the classroom teaches a worldview both explicitly and implicitly since, and as previously stated, experience is fundamental.

This chapter and the three that follow will examine the major worldview questions.

- What is the nature of reality and the universe?
- What is the source of knowledge and how does one know it is true?
- What is of value, right and wrong, and what determines it?
- What defines us as humans? What is our nature and purpose?

The Concept of God

"The key to any philosophy of life is one's concept of God: who He is, what He has done, and what His relationship is to the world and the people He created. . "Christian philosophy is the romance of seeing all things as one whole with God as the ultimate."[17] A worldview has a focal point and in the case of a Christian worldview the focal point is transcendent or other-worldly.

Fakkema's reference to "ultimate" implies that God is the reference or coordination point for all things.   God is the reason or purpose of everything else. The apostle Paul wrote of this truth in his letter to the Romans. "For from Him and through Him and to Him are all things" (Romans 11:36a).

To the Corinthians he emphasized the centrality of Jesus Christ as the foundation upon which he built his life, but also upon which others must build theirs. ***"For no man can lay a foundation other than the one which is laid, which is Jesus Christ"*** (1 Corinthians 3:11).

SO TOO, CHRISTIAN EARLY EDUCATORS WILL START WITH GOD AND REVEAL HIM THROUGH HIS CREATION, SCRIPTURE AND IN THE PERSON OF JESUS CHRIST.

An example of the impact of the centrality of God within an early childhood classroom has been an important part of my personal "God story". As I was completing my master's degree at the University of Texas, my wife and I were earnestly seeking our next place of service within the rapidly expanding Christian school movement.

At that point our understanding had been shaped by our shared experience as teachers in a missionary school in Korea, where regardless of the differences in denominational backgrounds, the emphasis was on Jesus and a shared desire to not only introduce students to Him but teach or disciple them through God's word. Several weeks before my graduation from the University of Texas, Linda invited our next-door neighbor to attend a Christian Women's Club luncheon.

The luncheon would hopefully serve as a door opener to sharing her faith. During that conversation our neighbor asked Linda what our plans were for the future and Linda shared what was a simple explanation of our emerging philosophy of Christian school education. Our neighbor's response was not only a surprise, but used by God to direct our future.

She said, "I went to a school like that when I was in first grade. You keep talking about God and so did everyone else in that school." Here was a young lady that to our knowledge at that point was not a believer, and yet during first grade experienced an unforgettable learning community where God was ultimate. Even more surprising was her suggestion that I send a resume to Norfolk Christian School in care of the founder, John Dunlap, at the corner of Granby and Thole Street.

I WAS SO CONVINCED THAT GOD BROUGHT THOSE DETAILS TO HER MEMORY THAT I DID AS SHE SUGGESTED AND WITHIN WEEKS I WAS IN NORFOLK FOR AN INTERVIEW BECAUSE IT "JUST SO HAPPENED" THAT THEY WERE SEEKING AN ADMINISTRATOR FOR THEIR PRIMARY AND EARLY CHILDHOOD UNIT.

I remember a conversation with my wife after my first day of interviews. I told her that it was indeed "our philosophy" in practice and within a couple of months we were on the road to Norfolk in preparation for the fall term.

The former headmaster and board chair of the school was Dr. Gene Garrick and he, as was his practice, made sure that every teacher understood the biblical distinctives of a Christian school. A notebook of his personal notes and outlines are on my desk as I pen these words. His wife shared his notes with me soon after he went home to be with Jesus. Throughout the pages of this book I will be sharing quotes as a means of sharing his teaching with a new generation of teachers.

I refer to this as a part of my "God Story" for a reason.

In Psalm 78 we are commanded to tell the next generation the "...praises of the Lord, and His strength and His wondrous works that He has done" (verse 4).

Too often we limit the stories of God to the works done in and among the people of Israel and the early church, but like them we should tell of the works He has done for us as well. Our personal stories, the stories of His daily presence and answered prayers, bring His presence into the classroom.

If God is to become the answer to the questions regarding the nature of reality, then we have to speak and demonstrate the reality of God in our own lives. As teachers show regard for him, refer to Him, sign praises to Him and lead the class in talking to Him, the foundation for "putting their confidence in Him and not *forgetting* the works of God" (v.7) is laid.

WHEN TEACHING WORLDVIEW, IT IS IMPORTANT THAT WE KEEP A CHILD'S LANGUAGE DEVELOPMENT AND WAYS OF THINKING (COGNITIVE DEVELOPMENT) IN MIND. THIS SHOULD NOT BE REASON TO SHY AWAY FROM PHILOSOPHY AND THEOLOGY, BUT IT IS REASON TO IDENTIFY TRUTHS THAT CAN BE MADE MEANINGFUL THROUGH EXPERIENCE (PAST AND PRESENT) AND AGE APPROPRIATE LANGUAGE.

Some examples, related to each of the four primary worldview questions, will serve as a starting place. Children will of course add their own questions and it is their questions that will not only be meaningful to them but give insight into their thinking and understanding.

The Questions Regarding Reality:

Is there a god?

Is there only one god or are there many gods?

God is in heaven and He is in our classroom. He is present because He is at all times in all places. God has given a book, called the Bible, about Himself and what He has done and is doing. As we hear His stories and words we will get to know Him better. In the Bible God is referred to as our Father, the Lord, King of Kings and Savior. He is the one and only true or real God. "God is one God, and God is three persons in an everlasting relationship with one another..."[18] He has always been and will be God forever and ever.

Sometimes people talk to or worship gods made of wood and stone. These made up gods are called idols. Anything that we think is more important than God, like toys and computers, can be an idol. God hears us and wants us to talk to him through prayer.

WHEN WE PRAY WE CAN TALK WITH HIM LIKE WE TALK

TO OUR PARENTS AND FRIENDS IN THE CLASSROOM.

Because He is God we will worship Him by obeying Him, singing songs and saying thank you for watching over us and caring for us.

What is God like? Where is He?

Because He is God there are many things that we may not understand but God has told us about Himself in the Bible and He sent His son Jesus to live on earth so that we could understand more about what He is like. His son's name is Jesus. He also sent the Holy Spirit to teach us about God. Jesus and the Holy Spirit are God. Some things, like God being three persons (Father, Son and Holy Spirit) are a mystery.

BUT SINCE GOD IS GOD IT SHOULD NOT SURPRISE US THAT SOME THINGS ABOUT HIM ARE DIFFICULT TO UNDERSTAND.

The Bible tells us that God knows everything; that He is good all the time; that He cares for (does good things) and watches over us; that He loves us and wants us to know Him and be friends with His son, Jesus. God does not like it when we disobey Him or do things that are wrong and He wants us to tell Him what we did, tell him we are sorry, and ask His forgiveness.

Even though God is present in all places, His throne is in heaven. Heaven is a real place where people who know God and allow Jesus to be the boss of their life will someday go to live with Him. The Bible describes heaven as a beautiful, peaceful place where there is no more sadness.

How did this world come into being?

God made the world and all that lives in it by speaking. He said, "Let there be" and it was. In this way He made the sun, moon, stars, the earth, oceans, plants, animals and you and me. This is why we also call Him the Creator. God designed everything to fit and work perfectly together. His creation shows us that God is really amazing and He and His words are powerful.

Are the things I can touch and see the only things that are real?

There are things that we have never seen or touched that are real. This includes an unseen world. There are many things that are so far away in space that we cannot see them, but they are surely there. Heaven is an example. God's book, the Bible, tells us that this is true.

From a developmental perspective, children are by nature open to God as a reality. Zuck and Clark refer to Piaget's reference to a child's creative, imaginative thinking and magical explanations. [19] This is displayed, for example, through their invention of supernatural persons and events. This means that the belief in Santa Claus and tooth fairies is without a need to prove existence. One might even say they have faith that there is a tooth fairy and that he or she will pay a visit. This example of childhood's way of thinking likewise opens a window of opportunity for belief in God as well as the idea that if God is God then He could at the same time be one God and three persons.

THE DAY WILL COME WHEN EVIDENCE AND RATIONALITY WILL ADD TO THEIR FAITH, BUT DURING THE EARLY CHILDHOOD YEARS, AN INTRODUCTION TO GOD, ALONG WITH THE OPPORTUNITY DURING EARLY CHILDHOOD TO EXPERIENCE HIM, IS ALL THAT IS NEEDED.

Attempts to separate fantasy and reality would prove futile, but what is possible is the identification of a dependable nurturing environment with a God who loves and cares for them. An ongoing exposure to teachers that model a mature faith in God will assure them of the reality of God.

A child's need for safety is critical to their social development. This need can likewise serve as a window of opportunity to acknowledge God and trust in Him. Lillian Katz, former professor of early childhood and director of the ERIC/ECE Clearing House at the University of Illinois, researched the needs that are basic to optimum social development.[20]

She synthesized the research into seven common experiences of children who are characterized as having "wholesome" development. When addressing her first proposition, the need to have a deep sense of safety, she wrote:

'I am referring here to psychological safety, which we usually speak of as a sense of "security" ...By psychological safety I refer to the subjective feeling of being connected and attached to one or more others. Experiencing oneself as attached, connected---or safe---comes not just from being loved, but from feeling loved, feeling wanted, feeling significant, etc. Note that the emphasis here is more on feeling loved and wanted than on being loved and wanted' (p.16).

The desire for and assurance of safety and security, though critical during early development, is not outgrown. In light of this it is not surprising that God addresses safety throughout Scripture. The Psalms in particular refer to God as the one that can and does provide for this need.

"In peace I will both lie down and sleep, for You alone, O Lord, make me to dwell in safety" (Psalm 4:8).

God is our refuge and rock (Psalm 18:2, Psalm 71) and his wings provide shelter (Psalm 36:7, 61:4, 63:7).

With God as our shepherd, what is there to fear?

We likewise are given the assurance that nothing can separate us from the love of God in Christ Jesus (Romans 8:39) and when we belong to God nothing can snatch us from his hand (John 10:28).

Children feel safe in their parent's arms or within the security of their rooms and we all find rest and security in Jesus's assurance that He is preparing a place for believers in heaven (John 14:2).

THESE TRUTHS WILL NOT ONLY REVEAL GOD'S NATURE, BUT ALSO, HIS POWER AND TRUSTWORTHINESS.

This understanding can serve as a motivation to seek and trust in Him for their safety both presently and in the future.

Immersion within a community where God is the focal point supports the emergence of faith during the impressionistic stage of faith development. Through the classroom environment, worldview integration and the incarnational life of the teacher, the children develop their initial answers to the worldview questions related to reality.

CHILDREN WILL ALSO EXPERIENCE THE MEANS TO CHRISTIAN EDUCATION'S CHIEF GOAL, THAT THEY MIGHT KNOW, LOVE AND GLORIFY GOD.

Extending Knowledge and Beliefs into Practice

1. Create a thematic unit centered upon the days of creation and God as creator. Focus on each day of creation through observation, crafts, creative arts etc. Interact with the children one on one throughout the study and remind them that because God loves us He made these things for us to enjoy and care for.

2. Provide a permanent bulletin board centered upon God as Creator. Use the bulletin board to portray the days of creation, the design, patterns, creativity and beauty found in creation.

3. Use story as a primary instructional strategy.

   Include:

   a. Stories about God's power over creation and Jesus' miracles
   b. Stories that illustrate what God is like
   c. Your stories about what God has done and is doing in your personal life

4. Speak with God through prayer. Incorporate regular as well as spontaneous times of prayer. Be sure to model statements of praise and gratitude. Make notes regarding prayer requests and be sure to refer to God and His love and care as prayers are answered.

5. Practice joyful and active times of worship.

   Design chapels for early childhood groups as opposed to bringing the young children to chapels where upper grades are also present. Limit "large group" chapels to holiday celebrations and other special occasions.

6. Create and maintain disciplined, safe learning environments. There should be several important classroom rules that can lovingly and consistently be addressed.

   Teach the children why the rules are important and explain the consequences not only for the child but others when rules are not followed. In so doing children learn to obey parents and teachers as the starting point for obeying God.

7. Speak of heaven not only as God's dwelling place but where those who love Jesus will someday go to be with him. In heaven there will be no need for the sun or moon because God's presence will give light. The walls of the city will be filled with jewels and the streets will be gold. There will be no more sorrow or tears.

8. Share or Integrate Children's Literature into your Bible lessons and shared reading times.

   a. Bohlmann, Katherine. 2002. *Grandma, what is Prayer?* St. Louis: Concordia.

   b. Bohlmann, Katherine. 2001. *Grandpa, Is There a Heaven?* St. Louis: Concordia.

   c. Bonner, Susan. 2012. *My Whole Self Before You: A Child's Prayer and Learning Guide Modeled after the Lord's Prayer.* Traverse City, Michigan: Kid Niche Publisher.

   d. Cole, Henry. 1995. *Jack's Garden.* New York: Greenwillow Books. (when reading to children insert the phrase "that God made" in regard to the earth).

    e. Groth, Jeanette. 1986. *Prayer: Learning How to Talk to God.* St. Louis: Concordia.

    f. Hoberman, Mary Ann. 1978. *A House is a House for Me.* New York: New York. Puffin Books. (when reading to children include heaven as our eternal home at the end of the book)

    g. Marxhausen, Joanne. *Heaven is a Wonderful Place.* St. Louis: Concordia. *This is also useful in learning about the nature of man.*

9. Memorize what the Bible says about God.

When selecting verses slight paraphrases may be needed to allow for better understanding. These and subsequent verses in the chapters that follow can serve as a Bible Memory Worldview Curriculum

    a. *In the beginning God created the heavens and the earth. Genesis 1:1*
    b. *God saw all that He had made, and it was very good. Genesis 1:31a*
    c. *All things were made through God, and without Him nothing was made. John 1:3*

    d. *For by Him all things were created that are in heaven and that are on the earth, the things that are visible and the things that are invisible. Colossian 1:16*
    e. *He gives to all life, breath, and all things...for in Him we live and move and have our being. Acts 17:28*
    f. *The earth is the Lord's and all it contains. Psalm 103:19*

g. *But our God is in heaven. He does whatever He pleases. Psalm 115:3*
h. *(God said) For I am God, and there is no other; I am God, and there is no one like Me. Isaiah 46:9*
i. *God is light and in Him there is no darkness at all. John 1:5*
j. *The eternal God is your refuge (safe place). Deuteronomy 33:27*
k. *The one who does not love does not know God because God is love. 1 John 4:8*
l. *Holy, holy, holy is the Lord God Almighty, who was and is and is to come. Revelation 4:8b*
m. *"You shall have no other Gods before me." Exodus 20:3*

Desiring God ministries has developed a resource to teach God's attributes to children. An attribute for each letter of the alphabet is presented as a series of lessons.[21]

10. Integrate children's worship songs into lessons and times of worship. This listing includes many well-known standards. The lyrics and videos are easily accessed through YouTube and online searches. Songs with movement add impact and facilitate the child's memory of the lyrics. Add your own favorites based upon whether or not the lyrics answer questions related to reality.

    a. He's Got the Whole World in His Hands
    b. What a Mighty God We Serve
    c. God is Good All the Time
    d. God of Creation (Mary Rice Hopkins)
    e. How Great is Our God
    f. The Lord is My Rock
    g. Our God is an Awesome God
    h. The Trinity Song, Folker

i.   My God is So Big
j.   My Father's House
k.   Jesus Loves Me
l.   Praise Him, Praise Him All Ye Little Children
m. God is So Wonderful (Parker Stephens)
n.   I want to Praise you for My Voice (iCharacter)
o.   My God is So Big and So Strong and So Mighty
p.   I Have a Friend Who Really Loves Me

Reflect and Respond

Education must be centered in Reality: God-centered/Christ-centered. To leave God (Christ) out is to misunderstand reality and life and purpose. Teachers must have this world-view if he or she is to teach from it. The chief GOAL of education is that the student might know and love God. H. Gene Garrick.[22]

1. Step back and "frame" or take a look at the classroom. In what ways does the classroom environment reflect God? Now consider the classroom with children present. Apart from direct instruction, in what way do the classroom interactions reflect the presence of God?

2. Evaluate the Bible curriculum in light of the question of reality? Is this worldview truth being taught? If so, provide specific examples. Is there a need to supplement the current curriculum?

3. Reflect upon your personal "God Stories". What stories have you shared with the children? Identify additional stories. Think about a personal God story that aligns with a Bible story that is being taught. Examples: A Story about personal healing, when God led or showed the way to go, when He gave strength and motivation to do something difficult, when obedience brought joy, when a hard time was a blessing etc.

4. Examine the nature of your early childhood worship time. Are these times of joy and engagement on the part of children? What can be done to better practice the presence of God and demonstrate praise and thanksgiving to Him?

5. In what ways are you assessing whether or not the children are developing an understanding of God as reality? What are they able to tell you about God at the end of their time in your preschool / kindergarten program? Means include interviewing, asking parents during a parent conference what their children are saying about God, keeping an anecdotal record of comments that children make in class etc.

Chapter Four: Worldview Integration: Knowledge and Truth

Sanctify them through Thy truth; Thy word is truth.

John 17:17

All Scripture is breathed out by God and profitable for teaching, for reproof, for correction, and for training in righteousness.

2 Timothy 3:16

Jesus said, "I am the way, the truth and the life.

John 14:6 ESV

Blessed are those whose way is blameless, who walk in the law of the Lord! Blessed are those who keep his testimonies, who seek him with their whole heart, who also do no wrong, but walk in his ways! You have commanded your precepts to be kept diligently. Oh, that my ways may be steadfast in keeping your statutes!

Psalm 119:176 ESV

- **WHAT IS TRUTH?**

- **WHAT CAN WE KNOW?**

- **HOW CAN WE KNOW?**

These questions must be raised by any philosopher. This may be the most important problem in philosophy. Unless it is possible to possess knowledge and to know the truth, it would be impossible to construct, let alone be sure of, any system of thought." [23] Gene Garrick

THERE ARE THREE OPTIONS WHEN ANSWERING THE QUESTIONS REGARDING THE SOURCE OF TRUTH---NATURE, MAN OR A TRANSCENDENT REVELATION (GOD).

Having established the Lord God as the ultimate reality and one in whom we can trust, it follows that whatever He would say would be true. Speaking falsely would disqualify God of His worthiness to take his place on the throne of heaven and earth. God has spoken and recorded His desires, commands, and redemptive plan in a book---the Bible. Holmes offered these reasonable assumptions, "God reveals Himself to men created in His image...This revelation is general---in creation; it is personal ---in Jesus Christ; it is written and propositional ---in the Bible...All truth then is God's truth."[24] Since God reveals truth through nature or creation (general revelation), it is said that God authored two books---The book of creation and the Bible.

Additionally, He revealed, through the incarnation, the Truth in the person of Jesus Christ His Son (John 1:14).

Responding to The Questions Regarding Truth:

Can we know what Truth is?

The truth can be known by reading God's Word, believing it, obeying what God says and listening to and doing what Jesus, God's Son, says and does (John 8:31-32).

Is there one Truth or are there many different truths?

God has told us the truth and Jesus did what was true because "He is the truth…" (John 14:6). There can only be one Truth. It could not be true if other ideas, those different from God's, were also true. If for example God says that He alone is God and someone else says there are many gods, then one of the statements must be false. God's word has been written down, and since God said it, it will always remain true no matter what.

What are the sources of Truth?

In addition to what God has told us in the Bible and what we see in the world He has made, Jesus is the Truth. Jesus is God's son and the Bible says that "all the treasures of wisdom and knowledge are hidden in Christ" (Colossians. 2:3), and that grace and truth came through Jesus Christ (John 1:17). Therefore, Jesus's words and teachings were true (John 8:45-46); His actions or behaviors were true (John 5:17) and His character (John 7:18) and relationships were true.[25]

God also has given the Holy Spirit to guide us to the truth. The Spirit teaches us and helps us to understand and remember what is true and what is not true (John 14:26). It is the Holy Spirit that guided the people when they first wrote God's Word. The Holy Spirit gave them God's thoughts and truths so that we too can know them. Both Jesus and the Holy Spirit are one with God and as such the source of all Truth is found in the Trinity.

The creation and how it works (creation laws) can be known through careful observation and when we study science. For example, when water is 32 degrees or lower it turns into ice. When water becomes really hot it turns to steam, it evaporates, and this water when it gets cool again turns back to water and returns to the earth as rain. The laws of nature are true and keep the world working in a perfect way. When God spoke the world into being God said that it was good, and the laws of science are part of that goodness.

God's Special Book

Because the Bible is a book authored by God, through the inspiration of the Holy Spirit, it should be viewed within the classroom as a special book. Young children will develop this disposition through the modeling of the teacher. The Bible should have a special place within the classroom. It is not placed randomly on the teacher's desk or bookshelf and it is handled with the respect and care that is becoming of the Truth. Whenever telling a story or teaching a truth from its pages, children should be reminded that it is a true story or that God is telling them what He wants them to know.

If God is talking then they should be encouraged to listen carefully because everything He says is important. Children should be taught that reading the Bible and memorizing its words are another way (in addition to prayer and worship) to spend time with Him and show their love for Him.

The Bible should also be viewed as a special book because God desires that the Truth be obeyed. Therefore, Bible lessons should end with the question, "What is God asking us to do?"

TOO OFTEN THE SOLE OBJECTIVE FOR A BIBLE STORY OR LESSON IS A DESIRE FOR THE CHILDREN TO RETELL THE STORY OR RESTATE A COMMAND LIKE, "HONOR YOUR MOTHER AND FATHER".

Using the example of honoring, a good portion of a lesson should center on what a boy or girl who demonstrates honor does. This is important if the child is to develop the habit of responding to the Truth. A heartfelt desire to obey on the part of the child must be accompanied by understanding what God desires and then imagining or planning ways to respond. The children should be led in a discussion of the ways in which they can honor their parents. Their responses might include ideas like, do what they say without fussing, thank them for their care, speak in a loving way and offer to help them.

If helping them is a suggestion then that should be followed up with the ways in which they might help, including role playing a situation where help might be welcomed by the parent. They should also be led to consider what <u>not</u> honoring would look like.

WHAT MIGHT A BOY OR GIRL DO THAT WOULD DISHONOR PARENTS? SHOWING WHAT DOES AND DOES NOT FIT A CONCEPT IS AN IMPORTANT ASPECT OF CONCEPT FORMATION.

When integrated into one's life the Truth becomes meaningful as opposed to abstract and this is especially important for a preoperational thinker and his or her faith development and spiritual formation.

The Creation "Book"

God's creation "book" should also be viewed with awe. God has revealed Himself through this "book" as well (Roman 1:20-24). The creation ordinances (laws of nature) should be studied through observation along with the continual reference to God's love as demonstrated through the world He has made.

Simple classroom science experiments, nature walks, and field trips to children's interactive museums provide the opportunities to point out God's "intelligent design". Children should be led to respond to His wisdom through praise and worship and through obeying God's command to care for creation.

Show them how to care for their immediate environment by providing opportunities to demonstrate stewardship of God's creation.

THROUGH THESE MEANS, TRUTH IS IMPACTING THE CHILD RATIONALLY, EMOTIONALLY, AND ACTIVELY THROUGH INDIVIDUAL INVOLVEMENT.

The overarching goal is that children simply see truth as originating in and revealed by God in creation and the Bible so that the foundation for the declaration that "All truth is God's Truth" becomes a part of the child's emerging worldview.

Extending Knowledge and Beliefs into Practice

- Take seasonal nature walks and provide a science exploration activity center

- Do simple science experiments and predict what will happen? Explain that we can know what will happen because of the creation laws (truths) that God created. For example, the children can plant seeds, but it is God, through his design, that provides water through the rain, light from the sun, and nourishment through the soil. Through God's provision he creates the flowers—all according to plan.

- When planning Bible instruction be sure to not only plan for response but imagine ways in which the children might respond. Guide them through the process of coming up with their own ideas of how they might respond. Think about your own response to the truth found within God's word and be ready to share what you have already done or will do in response to God. Should the children not offer a response, then be ready to provide a suggestion.

- When telling a Bible story hold an open Bible, if available and your hands are free, as a reminder that you are telling a story from the Bible. Emphasize that these are stories that really happened (true stories), tell them where the story is located, and begin by saying, "the Bible says....".   Select stories that focus on their aspects of their developing worldview and their moral and character development (discussed in more detail in the next chapter)

- On occasion make statements like, "People are saying that we can do whatever we want to as long as most of the people would agree that it is OK". Follow the statement with, "Is this true?" It is important that they begin to understand that just because people agree with something that does not make it true. Also ask, "How can we check to make sure that something is true?"

- Provide a Truth board. This bulletin board should post, in addition to a current memory verse, an additional statement of truth. Ideally locate this board where parents, in their coming and going, are likewise exposed to God's word and also have opportunity to know and support what the children are being taught. If teaching in a culturally diverse classroom post verses not only in English but also in the "heart" (or first) language of the children and their parents.

- Memorize what the Bible says about Truth. When selecting verses slight paraphrases may be needed to allow for better understanding.

  o *"Sanctify them through Thy truth; Thy word is truth." (John 17:17)*
  o *"This God—His way is perfect; the word of the Lord proves true... (Psalm 18:30a ESV)*
  o *"But he said, "Blessed rather are those who hear the word of God and keep it." (Luke 11:28 ESV)*
  o *Jesus said.... "I am the way, and the truth, and the life. No one comes to the Father except through me." (John 16:13 ESV)*

- o *"…. your word is truth, and every one of your righteous rules lasts forever." (Psalm 119:160 ESV)*
- o *Jesus said, "Heaven and earth will pass away but my words will not pass away." (Mark 13:31 ESV)*
- o *Jesus said, "If you stay in my word, you are truly my disciples, and you will know the truth…" (John 8:31 ESV)*
- o *You are near oh Lord and all your commandments are the truth. (Psalm 119:151 ESV)*
- o *"Everyone then who hears these words of mine and does them will be like a wise man who built his house on the rock." (Matthew 7:24 ESV)*

- Children's worship songs can be integrated into Bible lessons and times of worship. Also integrate, when appropriate, a song into the other disciplines i.e. build block houses on carpeted floor vs. a hard floor and explore the stability of the structure during a "STEM" lesson.

  - o The Wise Man Built His House Upon the Rock
  - o The B-I-B-L-E
  - o Check out the DLTK- Bible website for a listing of songs and poems about the Bible.[26]
  - o The Bible (Mary Rice Hopkins)

Reflection and Response

1. In what specific ways are you modeling the importance of the Word of God within your classroom?

2. Is the observation of God's creation (science) a regular part of your program? Consider not only what you are doing but what might be additionally done to share this source of truth with the children. How would your study of creation differ from that of those who view it through the lens of another worldview?

3. Reflect upon your recent Bible lessons. Identify the responses that children made to God's Word.

4. How would the understandings and suggestions within this chapter lay the foundation for a child's later understanding of the statement, "Truth from a biblical perspective is objective as opposed to subjective."

Chapter Five: Worldview Integration: Value

"Now this is the commandment, the statutes and the judgments which the LORD your God has commanded me to teach you, that you might do them in the land where you are going over to possess it, 2 so that you and your son and your grandson might fear the LORD your God, to keep all His statutes and His commandments which I command you, all the days of your life, and that your days may be prolonged. 3 O Israel, you should listen and be careful to do it, that it may be well with you and that you may multiply greatly..."

Deuteronomy 6: 1-3a

For the Lord disciplines those he loves, just as a father disciplines the son in whom he delights.

Proverbs 3:12

Children obey your parents in the Lord for this is right. 2 **"Honor your father and mother,"** which is the first commandment accompanied by a promise, namely, 3 **"that it may go well with you and that you will live a long time on the earth."**

Ephesians 6:1-3

Spiritual formation, as defined by Dallas Seminary, is

"THE PROCESS BY WHICH GOD FORMS CHRIST'S CHARACTER IN BELIEVERS BY THE MINISTRY OF THE SPIRIT, IN THE CONTEXT OF COMMUNITY, AND IN ACCORDANCE WITH BIBLICAL STANDARDS."[27]

THIS DEFINITION REFERS TO A PROCESS WHICH CAN AND SHOULD BEGIN IN CHILDHOOD, AND DEFINES THE GOAL AS HAVING THE CHARACTER OF CHRIST IN ACCORDANCE WITH BIBLICAL VALUES OR STANDARDS.

It also addresses the need for the work of the Spirit which aligns with the importance of leading a child to Christ as essential to beginning the process of spiritual formation.

The Bible, however, indicates a need to begin spiritual instruction prior to new birth. Parents, and teachers, are to place God's statutes upon their hearts, obey these commands and then "diligently" teach them to their sons and daughters.

IN OTHER WORDS, THE CHILDREN WERE TO BE GIVEN CONCRETE EXAMPLES OR MODELS AND TWENTY-FOUR SEVEN INSTRUCTION (DEUTERONOMY 6:4-9).

Morality and character are aspects of axiology or the study of values and addresses questions like:

- What is of value and how can we know what is right and wrong?
- What constitutes good and bad character?
- Who decides what is of value and beautiful?

Additionally, the Bible also speaks to addressing the heart as the source of one's behavior (Mark 7:21) along with the motivation for choosing right over wrong---the fear of the Lord (Proverbs 1:7).

God values the spiritual as opposed to the material and that which is eternal vs. the temporal (2 Corinthians. 4:18).

Since man is made in the image of God and God called it good (Genesis 1:26-27) his total person is of value. He has a moral nature and knows right from wrong (conscience).[28] Being made in the image of a relational God, relationship with Him and others is of greatest importance or value.

Sin has a direct impact on values---morality, ethics, and beauty. Because of sin people value self over God and personal desires over God's will and purposes.

> **WORLDVIEWS THAT EXCLUDE GOD AT THE CENTER END UP VALUING SELF-FULFILLMENT, AUTONOMY, HAPPINESS, MATERIAL THINGS, POSITION, POWER, AND SECURITY. THIS SHIFT IS REFLECTED IN CHILDREN WHO HAVE TOO OFTEN BEEN PLACED UPON PEDESTALS AND OVER INDULGED IN ORDER TO ENSURE THEIR HAPPINESS.**

Garrick (p. 38) provides a summary of the biblical alternative:

- **The possession of true life through sharing the life of God.** This was expressed by Jesus when he said, "What does it profit a man to gain the whole world and lose his own soul?" Redemption is to be valued above education.
- **Doing the Will of God.** The world passes away but he who does the will of God abides forever (1 John 2: 15-17).
- **Obeying the Law of God.** The law provides absolutes for behavior. These absolutes are not relative or subject to a majority vote (Matthew 5:17-19).
- **Sharing the Love of God.** Once God's love has been received it is then to be given back to God and others (Mark 12:30).
- **Thinking the Thoughts of God.** God's thoughts, which are higher than ours, contain the beauty of life. Beauty is found in what is "true, honorable, right, pure, lovely, of good repute, excellent, worthy of praise" (Philippians 4:8).

Responding to Questions Regarding Value

What is of Value?

Knowing God and belonging to Him is worth more than anything else in life. If we belong to Him He wants us to want what He wants and do what He would want us to do. The things of greatest value are related to God and His Kingdom which He tells us to treasure more than the things on this earth.

What is right and wrong?

Who decides and how can we know?

God tells us what is right and wrong in His word to us, the Bible. He gave us the ten commandments and also told us how we should live and treat others. The most important value is that we should love God and one another. God also shows us examples of people's right and wrong behavior in Bible stories. Man's ways are often sinful, but God's laws are right and for our good and our protection.

Do the rules (moral values and ethical standards) of right and wrong change?

God has not changed. He is good and Holy all of the time.   His desire for us to love Him and follow Him has not changed. The truths found in the Bible likewise remain unchanged. People may want to make changes to His laws but, like God, His Word endures forever.

Character Development: Pre-Operational Stage

Moral and character formation within early education classrooms begins with an understanding of how these aspects of development are unfolding in the child. Morality has both a cognitive and affective or social component. Moral theorist, Lawrence Kohlberg, applied Piaget's cognitive stages to moral thinking as the basis for his three stages of moral development.[29] Within each stage, there are two developmental levels.

The pre-conventional stage and the emergence of the first level of stage two, the conventional stage, occur during the early childhood years[30]. Since young children are concrete and fundamental in their thinking and learning, decisions of what to do, or a right vs. wrong choice, are directly tied to the child's perceptions of the consequences.

> **DURING EARLY STAGE ONE, THE CHILD IS PRIMARILY MOTIVATED BY A FEAR OF PUNISHMENT. THE NEED FOR PARENTAL DISCIPLINE AND CHILDHOOD OBEDIENCE IS THUS EMPHASIZED BY GOD IN SCRIPTURE (HEBREWS 12:5-6).**

William Damon believes that the child's relationship to authority is the "most important moral legacy" handed down by parents.[31] I have previously summarized Damon's characteristics of authoritative parents (and teachers) as those who:

> *Consistently enforce behavioural expectations, showing a commitment to their importance. Their commands are direct and honest, not indirect and manipulative. They value obedience and associate good behaviour with compliance with legitimate authority, and they confront students explicitly about any action that may harm (or negatively) impact others. In addition, Damon views induction as the most effective method of transmitting values.*

Induction is a technique for "ensuring the child's compliance through some form of control, but at the same time drawing the child's attention to the reasons behind the standard." [32]

During the second phase of stage one, motivation shifts from avoiding punishment to seeking a reward. The child now considers the positives that result from right behavior.

> THROUGHOUT THIS PHASE, BOTH COGNITIVE AND MORAL THINKING IS EGOCENTRIC. THE FOCUS OF THE CHILD'S THINKING IS ON "WHAT WILL HAPPEN TO ME?" EVEN DOING SOMETHING FOR SOMEONE ELSE IS A RESULT OF AN ANTICIPATED REWARD AS OPPOSED TO BEING MOTIVATED BY OTHER-DIRECTEDNESS.

Empathy or understanding the perspective of another is not yet fully present due to the cognitive limitations of preoperational thought. What may appear to be empathy on the part of the child may be a learned response to a stimulus within the context of his or her own past experiences and in this sense egocentric.

The child may be imitating the response an adult has made during a similar circumstance or a response that he or she might desire for his or herself in the same situation.

> THIS POINTS TO THE IMPACT OF IMITATION AND MODELING, BUT IT LIKELY DOES NOT, FROM A DEVELOPMENTAL PERSPECTIVE, REFLECT A RESPONSE BASED UPON AN *OTHER-DIRECTED* PERSPECTIVE OR THE CHILD'S HEART.

Right behavior is being learned, and behaviors or habits, regardless of the level of understanding, are the beginning of character in the child.

Character Development: The Conventional Level of Stage Two

Early spiritual development is directly related to the conventional level of moral thinking. Readiness for the gospel message involves an understanding of sin and that a consequence of sin is punishment.

Unless the child has experienced authoritative (love balanced with control) discipline, the understanding that a holy God must punish sin is not understood and the need for a Savior, who takes the punishment in his or her stead, is likewise not understood.

THE APPEAL OF HEAVEN AS A REWARD FOR RIGHTEOUSNESS ALIGNS WITH THIS THINKING.

CONSIDER JOHN 3:16 IN THIS LIGHT. "FOR GOD SO LOVED THE WORLD THAT HE GAVE HIS ONLY BEGOTTEN SON, THAT WHOSOEVER BELIEVES IN HIM SHOULD NOT PERISH (*PUNISHMENT*) BUT HAVE EVERLASTING LIFE (*REWARD*)."

This is often the initial motivation for response to the gospel during the early childhood years. It does not downplay the validity of the decision but shows an important link between moral thinking and spiritual formation.

It points to the importance of classroom discipline, an understanding of the concept of sin, the child's acknowledgment that he or she has sinned, the recognition of and acceptance of Jesus as Savior, and the subsequent reward of forgiveness, new life and an eternal home.

During the transition to concrete operations and the emergence of empathy in the child, more socio-centric behaviour begins. A feeling to please and be accepted as a good boy or girl becomes a motivating factor. There are rules of belonging, and to be accepted these rules are followed.

Even though there is a greater awareness of what others think, the motivation at this stage is, in the end, still self-serving. In spite of these limitations, the other-directed behaviours that characterize membership in the body of Christ can be taught and related to belonging to God and the church. The child's desire to be viewed as good by others can be related to God's wishes and that He too, like parents, has the expectation of right behaviour and is pleased by their obedience. Teachers must, however, caution against making a relationship with God based upon being a good boy or girl. The children must understand that Christ died for them while they were yet sinners (Romans 5:8) and that goodness is not a requirement for forgiveness.

RIGHT BEHAVIOUR MUST BE EMPHASIZED AS A THANKFUL RESPONSE TO GOD'S LOVE FOR US AS OPPOSED TO A MEANS OF EARNING GOD'S LOVE.

Throughout early childhood, teachers must remember that children are dependent upon fundamental learning experiences. This relates to the importance of modeling as a primary instructional tool. Children learn how to treat others and live together by watching how parents, teachers, and those more morally mature than themselves live other-directed lives. The behaviours between parents and children, and teachers and students are the primary moral lessons of early childhood. Children are also observers of how teachers within a school setting interact with one another. Robert Coles in his book on moral intelligence writes,

> *"moral intelligence isn't acquired only by memorization of rules and regulations, by dint of abstract classroom discussion or kitchen compliance. We grow morally as a consequence of learning how to be with others, how to behave in this world, a learning prompted by taking to heart what we have seen and heard. The child is a witness ; the child is an ever-attentive witness of grown-up morality—or lack thereof; the child looks and looks for cues as to how one ought to behave, and finds them galore as we parents and teachers go about our lives, making choices, addressing people, showing in action our rock-bottom assumptions, desires,*

and values, and thereby telling those young observers more than we realize.[33]

Too often character lessons within the Bible remain too abstract or removed from the child's world. As children begin to understand that Bible lessons should result in change and that changes are often linked to behaviour and how they treat others, they are taking the initial steps toward Christian character.

CHILDREN MUST NOT MERELY COME TO KNOW OR IDENTIFY A CHARACTER TRAIT (OFTEN AN ABSTRACT DEFINITION OR VERSE) BUT WHAT A PERSON OF CHARACTER DOES (THE CONCRETE OR EXPERIENTIAL MEANING).

The abstractions must be made meaningful by "converting nouns into verbs: tasks to accomplish, plans for action, to be followed by the actual work of doing" (p.16). For example, "Be kind and <u>compassionate</u> to one another" (Ephesians 4:32a). This mark of godly character must be translated or made concrete by the teacher of young children.

- What does a compassionate boy or girl do?

- What don't they do?

Compassionate children offer to help someone when they have fallen and are crying on the playground. They share their snack when someone has forgotten to bring one, and they want to help homeless people by bringing food during a collection for a local food bank. Those who are not compassionate laugh when someone falls, and they ignore the needs of others and don't offer to help.

Extending Knowledge and Beliefs into Practice

- *One's view of value affects all areas of education. There is no such thing as a value-free area of study. Biblical values, right and wrong, must be taught through the authoritative message of Scripture. Teaching, discipline, and modeling are the means of inculcating the tendency to act in accordance with God's moral law. Teachers must expose students to the good, limit exposure to evil and teach principles of choice. Children must be encouraged to think about their choices according to God's revealed will and standard. H. Gene Garrick*

- Be mindful of one's character and relationships within the school. Regular personal reflection and subsequent changes in behaviour are essential in light of the importance of modeling.

- Accountability partners are helpful as a means of not only identifying blind spots but taking the steps that lead to change and growth in one's character

- Create moral communities where authoritative discipline is practiced. Authoritative discipline is characterized by correction grounded in or balanced with love. Identify a set of classroom rules that can be consistently monitored and responded to when both followed and neglected. This requires a minimal number of clearly understood things that should and should not characterize student behaviour. **Caution should be taken to not overreact to childish irresponsibility or establish rules that are not developmentally appropriate, i.e. sitting still for extended periods of time.**

- Establish learning communities which include the parents. Parents are the child's primary teachers and models. Desired character traits, for example, should be acknowledged and supported by the parents through both their modeling and encouragement at home. Create a regular newsletter (email) or blog as a means of communicating the verbs that demonstrate or define the character traits being emphasized. Students imitate not only their parents and teachers but also the relationships between the two.

- Share stories that exemplify both right and wrong choices or behaviours. Bible stories and selections from children's literature that emphasize character provide opportunities to insert God's truth into follow-up conversations with the students. Some examples include:

  - Wilson, Karma. 2012. *Bear Says Thanks*. New York: Margaret K. McElderry Books. (Gratitude)
  - Becker, Bonny. 2008. *A Visitor for Bear*. Cambridge: Massachusetts: Candlewick Press. (Patience)
  - Children's books related to character are readily available online and can be used to locate additional books that related to a desired trait. One example is "Picture Books to Support Character Education.[34]

- Provide opportunities for the children to serve others. Nursing home visitations and performances, collecting food for the hungry within the community, showing gratitude to the firemen at a station serving the school, picking up classroom trash and wiping down tables at the end of the school day are some examples of other-directed behaviours. Also, consider family service opportunities where the children can work alongside their parents.

- Identify developmentally appropriate memory verses that reinforce the idea that character and values are determined by God and found in the Bible.

  - *(Jesus said) "You shall love your God with all your heart, with all your soul, and with all your mind. This is the first great commandment" (Matthew 22:36a).*
  - *...and the second is this. You shall love your neighbour as yourself" (Matthew 22:36b).*
  - *...What does the Lord your God require (expect) of you, but to fear the Lord your God, to walk in all His ways" (Deuteronomy 10:12).*

- o *(Jesus said)" ...if you want to enter into life, keep the commandments" (Matthew 19:17).*
- o *"...the one who does the will of God lives forever" (1 John 2:17b).*
- o The Ten Commandments
- o *"...now abides faith, hope, and love, but the greatest of these is love" (1 Corinthians 13:13).*
- o *Don't use bad language. Say only what is good and helpful to those you are talking to, and what will give them a blessing" (Ephesians 4:29).*
- o *"But seek first His kingdom and His righteousness, and all these things will be added to you" (Matthew 6:33).*
- o *"Fix your thoughts on what is true and good and right. Think about things that are pure and lovely, and dwell on the fine, good things in others" (Philippians 4:8).*
- o *"...put on a heart of compassion, kindness, humility, gentleness, and patience..." (Colossians 3: 12).*

Children's songs related to value:

- o Fruit of the Spirit (Kids Spring Children's Ministry)
- o The Perfect Ten (Katie Hill)
- o Love One another Lullaby (Dakota Pyle)
- o It is Good (Mary Rice Hopkins)
- o Kindness (Remba Kids)
- o Love Your Neighbour (Veggie Tales)
- o The Is My Commandment (Veggie Tales)
- o Wanna Be A Sheep (Mary Rice Hopkins)
- o Walk Like Jesus (Mary Rice Hopkins)
- o Sharing Comes 'Round Again (Mary Rice Hopkins)
- o God's Love (Mary Rice Hopkins)

Reflect and Respond

1. What are the enduring ideas (ideas at the heart of the matter and professional competency) found within this chapter?

2. Brainstorm the character traits that are or might be emphasized at each level of the early education program? Justify the reason why the traits would be both biblically and developmentally appropriate.

3. Examine your attitude toward discipline. Do you view discipline as a distraction or as a means for spiritual formation? Is discipline within your classroom authoritarian or authoritative? What is the difference?

4. To what degree are the parents involved as members of your moral community? What can be done to increase their involvement? Research conducted by Christian Smith in 2005 on the spiritual lives of teens found that the primary influencer was the parent. He concluded that the teens were not as influenced by culture as one might think but they were instead on track to become just like their parents. [35]

5. Reflect on the current effectiveness of your efforts toward moral and character development. What is the basis for your conclusion and how might you validate it?

Chapter Six: Worldview Integration: Humankind's Nature and Purpose

So, God created mankind in his own image, in the image of God he created them, male and female he created them.

Genesis 1:27

For all have sinned and fall short of the glory of God.

Romans 3:23

*Therefore, if anyone is in Christ, the new creation has come: The old has gone, the **new** is here!*

2 Corinthians. 5:17

You have searched me, LORD, and you know me. [2] You know when I sit and when I rise; you perceive my thoughts from afar. [3] You discern my going out and my lying down; you are familiar with all my ways.

Psalm 139:1-3

So, whether you eat or drink or whatever you do, do it all for the glory of God.

1 Corinthians. 10:31

> *"Man cannot be defined adequately as an animal, or as a social being, nor even as a rational being. He must be defined as the whole that he is, a spirit or person, or self whose normal and ultimate end is fellowship with God in the ultimate society of the many bound into the One."*[36]
>
> *J. Donald Butler*

The questions related to the origin of humanity, nature, and purpose complete the basic philosophical or worldview framework. It is critical that early education develop a proper understanding of humankind for two primary reasons.

THE WORLD PROVIDES CHILDREN WITH AN ARRAY OF MISCONCEPTIONS DURING A TIME WHEN A CHILD IS DEVELOPING HIS OR HER CONCEPT OF SELF.

Secondly, an initial understanding of self and one's place in the family and community is the centerpiece of a social studies curriculum during preschool and kindergarten.

Man, apart from the biblical perspective, is viewed as a "creature of biology."

> "Biological nature is human nature. Its conception of educational research is grounded in the faith that the scientific study of the human organism can give us all essential knowledge of human nature and behaviour---that is, knowledge not simply of man's biophysiological equipment, but also of his basic needs and powers, his primary likes and aversions, his drives, his enduring interests, and his invariant principles of growth and learning".[37]

Psalm 8: 3-6 presents the contrasting biblical viewpoint.

> *"When I consider your heavens, the work of your fingers, the moon, and the stars, which you have set in place, what is man that you are mindful of him, the son of man that you care for him? You made him*

a little lower than the heavenly beings and crowned him with glory and honour. You made him ruler over the works of your hands, you put everything under his feet."

A BIBLICAL WORLDVIEW DEFINES MEN, WOMEN AND CHILDREN AS DIFFERENT IN KIND FROM ALL OTHER ASPECTS OF CREATION---ANIMALS, VEGETABLE, AND MINERAL.

People are a higher form of life made in the image of God (Genesis 1:26-27) with the ability to think, act on his or her own (free will), communicate and organize. As an image bearer, every individual is both a personal being with a mind, emotions, will, and conscience and a relational being capable of fellowship with God and family.

As an image bearer, men and women reflect God passively or involuntarily like all of creation, but they, as stewards of the mysteries of God (1 Corinthians 4:1), are also free to choose and glorify God voluntarily, do His will, and have fellowship with Him.[38]

The image and nature of humans has been marred because of sin. Everyone has been given the ability to freely choose, but man did not obey God or choose to image Him. As a result, fellowship with God was broken.

INSTEAD OF A LIFE CENTERED UPON GOD'S WILL AND HIS PURPOSES FOR LIFE, THE FOCUS SHIFTED TO SELF AND LIFE INDEPENDENT FROM GOD.

Consequently because of sin, people are born with deceitful and wicked hearts (Jeremiah 17:9). In spite of man's fallen nature, scripture still refers to man as made in God's image (1 Cor. 11:7, James 3:9) because "he *(or she)* still has responsibility as God's image bearer and still retains his personhood in God's likeness... even though he has lost the image in his purpose"[39]

God Himself can only resolve the conflict between man as image bearer and as a sinner. It is not education alone that can address the problem and improve a man or woman's condition, but it is the restoration of man's relationship with God that is needed.

SALVATION IS, THEREFORE, THE FOUNDATION FOR SPIRITUAL GROWTH AND SHOULD BE VIEWED AS A CRITICAL SPIRITUAL OUTCOME WITHIN A CHRISTIAN PRESCHOOL AND KINDERGARTEN.

Responding to Questions Regarding Man

Where did we come from?

The Bible says that the first man and woman were created from the dust of the ground and that it was God that breathed life into them.

What are men and women like? How are they different from the rest of the things that God created?

Men and women, boys and girls, were created in the image of God. They are different from all the other things that God created. They can think, solve problems, create things, use a language to communicate with each other and with God.

THE BIBLE SAYS THAT EACH PERSON IS "WONDERFULLY MADE" AND KNOWN BY GOD FROM THE TIME THEY START TO GROW IN THEIR MOTHER.

Each person is different. They look and behave differently, but they all are equally important because they were all created by God to reflect Him. Each person even has a unique fingerprint. Each person has been given special talents and ways of thinking.

Why do people do bad things?

God gave people the ability to make choices. They are not like robots. They make choices about what they can and will do. They also decide what they do not want to do. Satan tempted Adam and Eve, the first man and woman, to not listen to or obey God. They chose to disobey God and have their own way. This wrong choice caused them to be separated from God.

Because of disobedience, sin entered God's created world and all people have had a sinful nature and sinned ever since. It is because of sin that people make bad choices and do bad things. It is because of sin that people die.

How does someone become a good person?

God loves all people, but people choose to do bad things. Because God loves his creation and especially people, he had a plan to deal with sin and restore relationships with people. This is good news, and this good news is called the Gospel. God sent his son, Jesus, to be punished for the sins of people. Since the punishment for sin is death, Jesus took our place and died for us on the cross. God offers people forgiveness as a gift. People cannot earn forgiveness, but they can accept the gift by believing what God did when Jesus died for them. When people accept this gift or offer of forgiveness, the Bible tells us that they are made new, it is like being born again. Their sins are forgiven, and they are now good in the eyes of God.

What does God want his people and children to do?

God desires that all people accept his free gift. He wants all people to know him, love Him, worship Him and serve Him. He wants them to love and care for others and tell them about God and His Son Jesus. The New Testament was written to tell people how they should live so that others can see an example of what God is like. He wants people to not only know His Word but also share what they learn with others.

What happens when someone dies?

People who trust in Jesus to forgive their sins go to heaven and live with Him forever when they die. People who have not been forgiven will be punished for their sins when they die.

A Child-Sensitive Orientation

An understanding of man, or in the case of early education, knowing the child must be at the heart of the teaching and learning process. Early educators are teaching children and not curriculum. A curriculum is a means to the end but, it is the children that do the work of learning. When considering a Christian view of man, early educators must also gain insight and understanding into a biblical view of the child—aspects of his or her nature and needs during early childhood.

It was at a parenting conference in Virginia Beach, Va. in 1976 when I was introduced to what would become a ministry life verse---Psalm 139:3. The speaker was "Buck" Hatch from Columbia Bible College, now Columbia International University. He asked the audience of young parents some facetious questions.

> "How many of you are here because you want to be the best parents possible?"

> "How many of you are willing to consider parenting your children the way your heavenly Father parents you?"

He proceeded to explain what he believed was the biblical starting point. Parents must become "intimately acquainted" (Psalm 139:3) with each child, their ways, their thinking, their talents, their temperaments, etc.

Not only must one become acquainted with their child's ways during their current stage of development, but also their ways along the continuum of development---infancy, early childhood, childhood, preadolescence, adolescence, and young adulthood.[40]

IT WAS AT THAT POINT THAT I CAUGHT THE VISION TO GET TO KNOW MY CHILDREN, BUT ALSO THE CHILDREN I WAS TO TEACH AND LEAD. TOO OFTEN TEACHERS STUDY CURRICULUM, DISCIPLINE, AND INSTRUCTIONAL STRATEGIES WITHOUT EVER BECOMING STUDENTS OF THEIR STUDENTS.

Children are always presented as immature and not mature in scripture. They must be taught everything, and their primary learning mode is experience and imitation. This means that worldview is learned through classroom experiences and observing the adults that surround them. Their thinking is fundamental and concrete which means that new concepts are developed through experiencing the concept.

Worldview truths too often remain abstract because the language surrounding the ideas have no experiential basis. Teachers must, therefore, keep in mind that worldview is being laid through what is done as opposed to efforts to explain it. It is the teacher talk that accompanies first-hand experiences that provides meaning. As children develop cognitively, ideas can be transferred through language because the vocabulary, through prior experience, has meaning.

It is this "way of thinking" that is referred to by Paul in his letter to the Corinthians. Children "speak like a child, think like a child, and reason like a child" (v. 11). They grasp parts, but it is not until later that they can see clearly. In light of this, an understanding of the nature of the student, and one's own nature, in particular, must be developed through the acknowledgment and celebration of differences.

IT IS IMPORTANT THAT TEACHERS ACKNOWLEDGE THAT EVERYONE IS ON AN INDIVIDUAL DEVELOPMENTAL TIMELINE SO THAT LATE BLOOMERS COME TO VIEW DIFFICULTY WITH A "NOT YET" AS OPPOSED TO "I CAN'T" VIEW OF SELF.[41]

Little children, by nature, are also dependent. They know that they cannot make it on their own and they look to parents and other care providers to meet their needs. Their dependence leads to a "faith" in their parents. Scripture refers to the child's faith as a model. It is not the child that should model adult faith but the adult that should have the faith of a child.

Early educators can guide children in the transfer of faith to God, the one who unconditionally loves them and will always care for them.

There should be a sense of urgency in that once a child reaches an age when independence is increasingly asserted, the transfer of faith becomes more difficult.

Teaching must strive to develop the student's potential as an image bearer. Their innate potential must be recognized, and creativity must be encouraged and maintained.

Every child can learn to communicate and read, but they may develop these abilities at different times through different means. Teachers can be confident of each student's literacy potential because they are created in the image of the Word.

They can also develop numeracy skills because they are created in the image of God the creator, the master mathematician, who created the world with such order that all of creation can be described mathematically.

Each child has been given ability, and early childhood classrooms should provide opportunities for the recognition of each child's special ability. It also provides an understanding that some tasks may be more difficult. They must come to know that being average is acceptable while at the same time recognize areas where they are truly above average. In so doing they will come to realize not just the truths concerning all persons, but also a knowledge of themselves.[42]

Extending Knowledge and Beliefs into Practice

Realize that developmental age varies as much as five years at age five. Some children may be a couple of years ahead while others may be one or two years behind in their development. This variance likewise varies within the child. For example, a child may be a year ahead in their language development while more than a year behind in their motor or social development. Teaching must be differentiated to maintain and promote the child's full potential and belief that they are capable learners.

Young children are creative and are anxious to show off their original creations. Unfortunately, by second grade most children have "lost" their creativity. This happens in part because of an emphasis on one right answer and craft projects where their products often, when following directions, look alike.

A CRAFT AND A WORK OF ART ARE NOT THE SAME THING.

Crafts are good tools to practice fine motor skills and following instructions, but early education classrooms should make sure that opportunities to be artistic and inventive are a regular part of the curriculum.

Extending Knowledge and Beliefs into Practice

- Create an authoritative classroom environment where love and control are in balance. Provide and consistently monitor a few important rules. When a child chooses to break a rule, provide the child with consequences. Discipline should include a child's admission that they chose to disobey followed by forgiveness and a new beginning (restoration). Children need to be shown, not only how to admit they were wrong, but also how to demonstrate that they are sorry for their actions.

- Teach children that prayer times are opportunities to fellowship with God

- Lead parents in having an honest understanding of their child's talents and abilities. Encourage the acknowledgment of their child's talent but likewise, help them accept areas where a child falls in that area called average.

- Begin the academic year with home visits and family picnics to get to know children and their backgrounds. Ask parents to tell them about your students—likes, dislikes, talents, etc.

- Study the cultures of students who are not from your cultural background. Always be mindful of the ways within a culture when interacting with children and their families.

- Avoid an overemphasis on "empty" praise. The words "good job" for example, lose meaning through overuse and more so when it is used to describe something that does not deserve it. Sometimes the words "good effort" is the more appropriate statement. Shift attention from end product to the process.
- Regularly provide opportunities to review the gospel. Pre-kindergarten and kindergarten is a time period in which children often accept Jesus as Saviour, or in cases of infant baptism begin to understand and embrace the meaning of baptism.

- Involve the children in developmentally appropriate service projects within the school and community. Bake cookies and deliver them to a nearby fire station. Visit a nearby facility for the elderly and allow the children to sit on the rug and play while the residents observe. Deliver a box of food to a food bank etc.

- Share children's literature about children who have overcome difficulties and followed and achieved their dreams.

- Start to develop the purpose of school as preparation for what God asks you to do as opposed to earning good grades and going to a good college.

Integrate Bible stories that can be used to emphasize that God has a plan for each of His children. Rick Warren, *the author of the Purpose Driven Life*, has created a storybook Bible using stories that emphasize how God wants us to live, and a desire to help children discover God's plan for their lives. Each of the stories concludes with biblical truth, a verse to remember and an application question. Many of the stories would likewise help in developing a biblical view of value.[43]

Memorize scripture that relates to our identity

- … *"So, God created man in his own image, in the image of God he created him; male and female he created them"* (Genesis 1:27).
- *"For we are his workmanship, created in Christ Jesus for good works"* (Ephesians 2:10a).
- *"I praise you for I am fearfully and wonderfully made. Wonderful are your works"* (Psalm 139:14).
- *"Fear God and keep his commandments, for this is the whole duty of man"* (Ecclesiastes 12:13).
- *"Many are the plans in the mind of a man, but it is the purpose of the Lord that will stand"* (Proverbs 19:22).
- *"All have sinned and fall short of the glory of God"* (Romans 3:23).
- *"For the wages of sin is death, but the free gift of God is eternal life in Christ Jesus our Lord"* (Romans 6:23).
- *"For God so loved the world, that he gave his only Son, that whoever believes in him should not perish but have eternal life"* (John 3:16).
- *"If we confess our sins, he is faithful and just to forgive us our sins and to cleanse us from all unrighteousness"* (1 John 1:19).
- *"The people whom I formed for myself will declare my praise"* (Isaiah 43:21).
- … *"your body is a temple of the Holy Spirit within you…* (1 Corinthians 6:19a).
- *"You are not your own, for you were bought with a price. So glorify God in your body"* (1 Corinthians 6: 20).
- *"If anyone is in Christ, he is a new creation. The old has passed away, behold, the new has come"* (2 Corinthians 5:17).
- "By this my Father is glorified, that you bear much fruit and so prove to be my disciples" (John 15:8).
- "Let everything that has breath praise the Lord! Praise the Lord!" (Psalm 150:6).

Sing truths related to aspects of God's mission, His nature, our needs and His purpose for our lives

- This Little Light
- John 3:16 Bible Memory
- The Butterfly Song (Piapena)
- A Gift to You (KWSCM)
- Create in Me (Mary Rice Hopkins)
- Don't Dig a Hole (May Rice Hopkins)
- Running for the Prize (Mary Rice Hopkins)
- God Made All of Me

Reflect and Respond

1. To what degree do your classroom practices recognize the uniqueness of each child? Think about your current students. What are some of the differences among the children? Make a list of each child's strengths, average abilities, and weaknesses? Is there an emerging talent?

2. Do you require students to verbally admit when they are wrong? The statement, "I'm sorry," should be followed with what they are sorry about and the words, "Will you forgive me?" Are you observing whether or not the child's body language and actions reflect contrition? Are you helping children to understand that anger is a natural response to some situations, while at the same time teaching them appropriate responses when angry?

3. How are you modeling a correct response to anger?

4. Do you give opportunities for children to regularly use and develop their distinctiveness as human beings? Identify ways in which you provide opportunities for them to be creative; to develop their language and communication skills; to solve problems on their own and develop their social or relational skills? What might you do differently?

5. To what degree are you intentionally offering meaningful praise?

Chapter Seven: The Redemptive Story

According to the grace of God given to me, like a skilled master-builder, I laid a foundation, but someone else builds on it. And each one must be careful how he builds. [11] For no one can lay any foundation other than what is being laid, which is Jesus Christ.

1 Corinthians 3:10-11

So, faith comes from hearing, and hearing through the word of God.

Romans 10:17

Whoever believes in the Son of God has the testimony in himself...And this is the testimony, that God gave us eternal life and this life is in his Son.

1 John 5:10-11

And that from childhood you have known the sacred writings which are able to give you the wisdom that leads to salvation through faith which is in Christ Jesus.

2 Timothy 3:15 (NASB)

What then is necessary for child conversion? The same thing that is essential in adult conversion: a conscious turning from sin and a turning toward God...Incline the child to put his faith in Christ by sound Christian teaching surrounded by Christian love from birth onward. Such pre-evangelism, as it may be called, builds a proper foundation for intelligent faith and active discipleship.

Edward L. Hayes [44]

Parents want the best possible future for their children, and so they seek the right early childhood program as a means to future success. They want children to have not only a good start, but a head start, to ensure the chances of good grades, high test scores, admission to the best colleges, and successful careers. This desire reflects "the pattern of this world" or the culture in which we live. From the perspective of a Christ-centered worldview, however, this future often lacks meaning, purpose, and preparation for eternity.

Ted Tripp in *Shepherding a Childs's Heart* points out that the orientation of a child's heart will be influenced to go in one of two directions. It will be directed either Godward or toward "things that are not God and that cannot satisfy." (p. 21)"[45] Children are either growing in their understanding of the implications of who God is, or they are seeking to make sense of life without a relationship with God...The question is not "will they worship?," It is always "whom will they worship?" (p.22) The home and school provide the "shaping influences," and the nature of this influence will flow from the worldview of the home and school.

IT IS THE PURPOSE OF THE CHRISTIAN SCHOOL TO NOT ONLY PREPARE THE CHILD FOR THIS LIFE, BUT FOR A LIFE WITHOUT END.

The answer to the question, "what will the children choose to do about Christ?" is the essential question.   In the same way that there is no neutral education; there is no neutrality when it comes to Christ.

The children will either come to know and follow him or continue to go their own way. The choice to believe in Jesus is the first and most foundational stepping stone along the path of spiritual growth and formation. It is for this reason that early education teachers must understand and provide the means to that first step---the Gospel of Jesus Christ.

The Christian Worldview Narrative

Younger children are egocentric and therefore see life from their perspective. At this stage in their life, it is not because they are self-centered, but because the ability to see things from another's perspective has not yet developed. However, it does, unless otherwise directed, naturally develop into self-centeredness. Early education teachers have the daily opportunity to focus the child's attention beyond themselves to God and others---from a narrow perspective to the grand narrative.

> **THROUGH INSTRUCTION AND MODELING, THE CHILDREN MUST BE**
>
> **INTRODUCED NOT ONLY TO THE STORY BUT TO THE IDEA THAT THEY ARE**
>
> **PART OF THAT STORY.**

All worldviews have a narrative. Valid worldviews have not only a story, but a story that provides a meaning and purpose for life. The story must be logical, consistent and worthy of placing one's faith in it. It must work. The biblical narrative is the only one, that upon close examination, meets the criteria.[46]

God's story is the basis for all other good stories. Stories contain the classic five acts as illustrated by Shakespeare's plays. "Listen in" as Lawrence and Nancy Goldstone discuss the story with children.[47]

"Shakespeare uses the first act," we say, "to introduce his characters, and then, in the second act, he throws them together and lets the conflict build. In the third act, the conflict boils over, the climax is reached, and the protagonist (and often the antagonist) is changed forever. In the fourth act, we see the impact of the climax on the characters, in in the fifth act, we find out what happens to everyone." (p. 60)

The Goldstones also identify the protagonist as the character in the story who is "trying to push the action forward" while the antagonist, a person or idea, tries to "hold the action back." This pushing backward and forward creates a conflict. When you identify these elements you "have come a long way to knowing what the story is about." (p. 26)

The story of God and His purpose for humans to reflect Him and fill the earth with His glory has all of the components.

God had a plan to create man and enter into a relationship with him (creation). God created humans as unique reflections of His glory and commissioned them to "be fruitful and multiply" and thus reflect His glory throughout the earth.

Satan, the antagonist, seeks to destroy God's plan and persistently tempts humans to rebel and abandon God's purpose for their lives through disobedience. The result is humans experience the consequences of disintegration and live in separation from knowing and having fellowship with God and others (the fall).

God, through His love and grace, revealed a plan to redeem lost sinners and bring them back to himself. The struggle between those who are living for the glory of God and those who are not unfolds across time.

Humans continually turn their backs on God and experience the consequences of their sin. While God continually, demonstrates grace and mercy and invites humans to repent and return to Him.

The story climaxes when Jesus, the centerpiece of God's plan, comes to perfectly reflect the Glory of God while humbling Himself and offering His life to redeem those living in rebellion to God and His purpose. This act of love culminates with Jesus' resurrection and victory over sin and death, the story continues as the impact of Jesus' life and death unfolds in the book of Acts and the Epistles and as the apostles take the good news of the resurrection throughout the world.

These ambassadors of the good news not only invite people to return to a restored relationship with God and His purpose for their lives, but to complete the original purpose of God for humans to fill the earth with the reflection of His glory both individually and through the church.

When people understand their invitation to participate in God's purpose for their lives, they realize that the story includes them and that they have a special part in God's ongoing story. The story of God promises that His purposes will be achieved and foretells our relationship with Him throughout eternity.

Teaching "One Story"

Barna has concluded that there are four "cornerstones" related to the formation of a spiritual champion." [48] The second cornerstone is a "commanding knowledge of biblical content," and cornerstone three is "the identification of organizing principles." A knowledge of the one story does not only satisfy the need for knowledge, ***but it is also a framework for organizing that knowledge***.

IT PROVIDES A MEANS OF TAKING THE PARTS OF THE STORY, TOO OFTEN TAUGHT IN ISOLATION AND OUT OF SEQUENCE, AND INTEGRATING THEM INTO A MEANINGFUL WHOLE.

Ed Stetzer in a Christianity Today article, expresses a concern which grows, in part, out of the fear that the Bible can become a group of "isolated morality tales, like Aesop's Fables." [49]

THIS TEACHING TOO OFTEN MERELY RESULTS IN A MODEL FOR RIGHT LIVING BASED ON GOOD AND BAD BEHAVIOUR AS OPPOSED TO THE TELLING OF THE BIGGER STORY THAT FORMS THE BASIS FOR TEACHING THE GOSPEL.

He goes on to state that children can miss the "plan that has been designed and implemented by a loving God for the saving of humans." Stetzer's explains:

…we hear Jesus say in 1 Corinthians 11, 'This cup is the New Covenant in My blood. Do this as often as you drink it in remembrance of Me'. However, we don't remember that Moses said, 'This blood is a symbol of the covenant' in the Old Testament. We don't understand why Abraham would be called to sacrifice Isaac if we don't understand what would happen as God the Son is sent by God the Father to be the perfect sacrifice for our sins. This interconnectedness happens all through Scripture.

Appendix B provides an outline of the redemptive story.[50] It is not uncommon to find teachers who are either not familiar with the idea of one story and may limit the story to the New Testament without its relationship to the Old. Naturally one can and will continue to teach Bible stories, but it is important that teachers also show a Bible story's relationship to God's bigger narrative. Within the outline, you will find intermittent samples of the redemptive narrative.

The language, written at a primary level, may need some modification for use at the preschool or kindergarten level. After becoming familiar with the framework, share each part of the story in the same way you would tell other stories within your classroom.

If you are unfamiliar with sharing The Story, I suggest you read Kevin DeYoung's beautifully phrased and illustrated book, *The Biggest Story* as means of introducing yourself to how the story might be told.[51] Appendix B also references Bible story books for young children. The locations (page numbers) of frequently used Bible stories that align with each portion of the redemptive narrative are also referenced in the Appendix B.[52]

The "One Story" provides the biblical context for the Gospel. All people at some point must hear and understand the Gospel if they are to believe. Chris Browne writes that "hearts of students must be assessed in order to equip teachers to connect to their hearts and differentiate their teaching to meet the individual spiritual needs of the students." [53] The spiritual needs differ according to stages of spiritual growth based upon soil as a representation of the hearts of people in the parable of the soil (Matthew 13:1-23, Mark 4:3-20 and Luke 8: 5-15).

Preparation for the Gospel

> ***"Spiritual growth is directly related to how an individual understands and responds to the Word of God"*** (p.41).

It is the Holy Spirit that prepares hearts and "God uses teachers in the process of equipping the student to hear, understand and respond to the Word of God" (p. 41).

It is the teacher that prepares the soil upon which the seed will be planted. Much of this book has been devoted to understanding the necessary "nutrients" within a rich soil. Enriched soil allows students to understand and connect with the message. Browne outlines six types of soil that can be aligned with six stages of faith.

His explanation also outlines the barriers to faith as well as the spiritual needs that characterize each stage as outlined and defined by Scripture. As early childhood educators, the first three levels most directly relate to the hearts and needs of the young child.

STAGES OF SPIRITUAL GROWTH (Browne, 2012, p. 43-46)				
	Description of the heart	Invitation from Christ	Barriers to Growth	Spiritual Needs
Skeptic	Calloused heart Deaf Ears Closed Eyes	Repent, Believe	Lack of spiritual understanding	Befriending by a loving and praying believing friend, A personal change of mind and heart initiated by the Holy Spirit
Seeker	Ready Heart Open Ears Questions	Repent, Believe	Lack of clear presentation of the Gospel, lack of an invitation.	Clear Gospel presentation and invitation to receive, believe.
Believer	Seed begins to germinate but soil is shallow, and there are little or no roots	Follow	Lack of roots, testing, trouble, persecution	Prayer, roots, knowledge, teaching, worship, time, someone to walk with them
Follower	Roots are beginning to push through the soil and struggle with thorns	Deny Self, Pick up Cross. Trust and Obey, Love Christ and others	Thorns, worries of this life, doubt, the deceitfulness of wealth, comfort, self	Deny self, trials, endurance, perseverance, time, small group relationships and accountability.
Friend	Good soil, obedient to Christ, Fruit	Love. Obey. Go	Complacency, fear, pride, lack of vision, lack of equipping	Continued obedience. Equipping, empowerment, continued spurring and accountability within a community
Fisherman	Good soil, fruit, harvest, influence. Reflect Christ	Teach Others	Complacency, fear, pride, lack of vision, lack of equipping, wariness.	Perseverance, humility, faithfulness, accountability, reliable people.

All early childhood programs are engaged in reading readiness.

WITHIN THE CHRISTIAN PRESCHOOL AND KINDERGARTEN, EVANGELISM READINESS SHOULD LIKEWISE BE OF CONCERN. EVANGELISM READINESS IS THE PREPARATION OF SOIL UPON WHICH THE SEED OF THE GOSPEL CAN BE SOWN.

Donald Joy writes, "Early, consistent saturation in a warm, Christian nurture environment helps children respond personally to Christ's call to salvation…a child's need is for a warm identification environment in which he *or she* may develop a strong sense that he is loved by God and by the Christians around him." [54]

Browne's first three stages characterize the young child.

IN TODAY'S CULTURE, THERE MAY BE MORE WHO ARE SKEPTICS WITHIN OUR EARLY CHILDHOOD CLASSROOMS THAN EVER BEFORE.

I believe there may be three reasons for this. If you rewind to the earlier decades of the modern Christian school movement, you would find, with few exceptions, that children enrolled in Christian schools were from believing homes.

Children came from an environment where nurturing had begun at birth. Secondly, even though children may not have had an early Christian nurturing, the parents, even though not Christian, were less likely to express bias against Christians and their beliefs. Many of today's children may be experiencing negative comments regarding the Bible and the church within their homes.

Comments like, "I don't believe in God" or "The Bible is a bunch of make-believe stories" may not only be overheard but directed to them. Since children are imitators, they too may be more skeptical. Thirdly, due to the increased frequency of verbal and physical abuse and neglect, the ability to trust may not be present.

TAKE NOTE OF THE SPIRITUAL NEEDS OF A SKEPTIC: "THE NEED FOR A LOVING, BELIEVING, PRAYING FRIEND AND AN ENVIRONMENT WHERE THE POSSIBILITY OF A CHANGE, THROUGH THE WORKING OF THE HOLY SPIRIT, IS A VERY REAL POSSIBILITY".

The seeker has moved beyond "closed ears and eyes" to being ready for a clear presentation of the Gospel and an invitation to believe. The context of the bigger redemptive story increases readiness to obey Jesus and follow Him. These young new believers will find nurture for their tender roots in distinctively Christian classrooms where teachers shepherd, worship, pray, teach and encourage them to trust Jesus and allow Him to "be their boss."

Sharing the Gospel

The actual presentation of the gospel should be at the child's level and taught in a simple, straightforward way. The language should align with the language of the gospel repeated throughout the redemptive story. Use the phrase "The Bible says" often within Bible stories and throughout the presentation of the gospel as well.

Share these truths:

- God loves you.
- He wants to be your friend, but you too have sinned and want your own way
- Christ died to pay for your sin and provide a way that your sins can be forgiven.
- Confess to God that you have sinned and ask for His forgiveness.
- Know that through His love and grace God has forgiven you, and if you believe God will do what he has promised, then know that He also welcomes you as one of his children.

These basic elements are often taught through instructional tools like the wordless book or bracelets. These and other gospel tools help the child link and remember the components of the gospel. The language of the presentation should be culturally responsive. For example, depending on the ethnicity of students, the representation of the color black with sin and white with the absence of sin may lack sensitivity and hinder the responsiveness of the child. An alternative approach may be the substitution of the wordless book's black page with a smudged white page and then, through the blood of Jesus, show a white page without smudges.

Consider the vocabulary that is used in presenting the gospel. Ask yourself, do the students know the meaning of the words I am using? Have I used this vocabulary regularly within in the context of my Bible teaching and within the redemptive narrative?

AVOID THE TENDENCY TO LINK BEING GOOD BOYS AND GIRLS TO BEING LOVED BY GOD.

Children are surrounded by expectations to be good. "Good job" has become a sort of mantra over recent years. Yes, right behavior is God's desire, but it is not the basis of His love.

MAKE SURE THAT GOD'S GRACE IS UNDERSTOOD THROUGHOUT THE REDEMPTIVE STORY. ALL BIBLICAL CHARACTERS WERE SINNERS, AND AS SUCH FELL SHORT.

Look for the grace and the foreshadowing of Jesus. Help children to understand the good news "God demonstrates his own love for us, in that while we were still sinners, Christ died for us". (Romans 5:8)

Teachers are God's mouthpiece, but teachers are not the ones responsible for the child's conversion. "We are to balance our zeal with confidence in a sovereign God. Faith comes by hearing and hearing by the Word of God (Romans 10:17)." [55]

TOO OFTEN AN APPEAL TO ACCEPT CHRIST CAN BE PUSHED UPON THE CHILD.

One needs to remember that the Gospel, when appropriately and clearly presented, has its own appeal, and the work of the Holy Spirit has its own power (p.161).

When offering an invitation or asking for a child's response, one should:

- Ask children to respond "inside" as opposed to an outward response. One might say to the children, "If you want Jesus to be your Savior, say to Him, Yes, Jesus I want You to be my Savior." Avoid group decisions.

- Encourage children to talk with you or their parents if they want Jesus to be their Savior. When they come, ask them why they came to talk.

Should a child say, "Can I accept the Lord or ask Jesus to be my Savior?" then that is an opportunity that should not be put off.

- Be mindful of statements like "ask Jesus into your heart," and other simplistic phrases that may lead to a decision that is not genuine or that is not even meaningful. For young children the phrase "ask Jesus into your heart," when taken literally, is a scary proposition and can be a detriment rather than an encouragement.

  Confession should be part of a child's response to the Gospel. Children often find it difficult to admit they are sinners or have disobeyed God. When under the authentic conviction of the Holy Spirit, they should be able to voice that they have sinned.

- They need not confess a specific sin to you but should be encouraged to tell God and ask for His forgiveness as part of their response to the Gospel.

Childhood transgressions within the classroom are teachable moments in that they provide opportunities to speak to the heart of the child. Some of these opportunities include lying, stealing, disobeying parents, jealousy, and causing pain through unkind words and actions toward other children.[56]

Discuss inappropriate behaviors with the child. Ask whether he or she has made a good choice or a bad one. Following the response, ask the child why the inappropriate behavior was a bad choice. Follow that with gently thinking through what might have been a better choice.

Be sensitive to the times when there is a heart response from the child and when the conversation may have opened the door for gospel truths. Make every effort to resolve a child's guilt through admission of their wrong behavior to both you and hopefully, God. Assure them that you have forgiven them and remind them that when we ask God, He will forgive as well.

Shortly after completing this chapter I read an online post from a former student at Columbia International University. Caleb is following his calling as a third-grade Christian school teacher. I believe his reflection provides the perfect conclusion for this chapter.

> *Today in class I felt led to share the Gospel for the 15th time (or more) this year and give an invitation. Two of my students decided to follow Jesus…that makes five in all this year. So many teachers are ready for the end of the school year and counting down the days. It's easy to give up at the end, but I'm kind of sad and trying to treasure every last minute I have with these kids.*
>
> *I've grown to love them so much, and many days I feel like I have the best profession in the world. I get to disciple kids and teach them about Jesus. I don't think you can find anything better to do with your time than that! "Be always abounding in the work of the Lord, knowing that in the Lord your labour is not in vain." 1 Cor. 15:58*
>
> *Caleb Hankin, Freedom Christian Academy, Fayetteville, NC*

Reflect and Respond

1. Consider the Bible curriculum that you currently use. To what degree does it provide the foundation for the Big Story? Are the individual stories sequential and held together under the theme of God's love (grace), promises and plan?

2. Think through the gospel narrative that you share with children. Is the language or story in alignment with the language presented by your Bible curriculum? Is it culturally responsive?

3. What is your response when there are authentic opportunities to invite students to believe and follow Jesus?

4. John Piper, in a message to his congregation, said, "Be like children in relation to God and be like God in relation to children." [57]. Explain your interpretation of this quote based upon your reading and understanding of this chapter.

Chapter Eight: A Living Curriculum

"Therefore I urge you, brethren, by the mercies of God, to present your bodies a living, and holy sacrifice, acceptable to God, which is your spiritual service of worship. And do not be conformed to this world, but be transformed by the renewing of your mind, so that you, may prove what the will of God is, that which is good and acceptable and perfect."

Romans 12:1-2

"However, you are not in the flesh but in the Spirit, if indeed the Spirit of God dwells in you. But if anyone does not have the Spirit of Christ, he does not belong to Him. If Christ is in you, though the body is dead because of sin, yet the spirit is alive because of righteousness."

Romans 8: 8-11

"Be imitators of me (Paul), just as I also am of Christ."

1 Corinthians 11:1

"There can be no Christian education without a Christian teacher."
Frank Gaebelein[58]

A question that I am often asked is, "what curriculum do you recommend?" Since the curriculum is the means to accomplish a program's desired outcomes, chapters three through six presented a faith-directed, Christ-centered curriculum. The curriculum is a classroom community where teachers acknowledge God's presence, present worldview truths and character standards established by God and found in the Bible, and where children are viewed as image bearers who are uniquely and wonderfully made.

THIS IS A LIVING CURRICULUM, AS OPPOSED TO A BOOK OR NOTEBOOK THAT OUTLINES DAILY INSTRUCTION.

This understanding of curriculum is especially important when considering the learning style or means through which the preoperational child learns. As stated throughout the book, this curriculum is experienced-based and under the moment by moment direction of a living, relational early childhood educator.

It is the teacher who has the mind of Christ and reflects a life in relationship with God. These teachers translate abstractions into experiences that are developmentally appropriate, understandable and transferable into the life of a young learner (Proverbs 27:27).

It is therefore impossible to conceive of early Christian education without teachers who have experienced rebirth and are committed to a life of learning, growing, following, and serving Christ. The life of the teacher demonstrates and validates the truths of the Bible (Matthew 7:20).

Christian teachers, as they walk in the Spirit, fulfill the role of a prophet when they witness to and teach truth from God's perspective (1 John 1:1-3). They serve as priests or mediators as they bring the student's needs to God and they serve as king through exercising their God-given authority as they guide and counsel students.[59]

The role and influence of the teacher bring a new level of understanding to James 3:1 where the reader is reminded that "...not many of you become teachers, my brethren, knowing that as such you will incur a stricter judgment."

Within the same chapter, there is also truth teachers can, through experience, validate— both the negative and positive impact of the tongue. The content and tone of verbal interactions create an atmosphere of encouragement vs. discouragement, joy vs. anger, peace vs. fear, and warmth vs. coldness.

The Example of the Apostle Paul

The apostle Paul understood the importance of modeling and accepted the responsibility. "Brethren join in following my example and observe those who walk according to the pattern you have in us" (Philippians 3:17).

Paul wept over the fact that <u>many</u> were walking in or demonstrating error as opposed to the truth because their god was their appetite and their minds were set on earthly things as opposed to a heavenly citizenship (v 18-20).

Paul not only referenced himself as "living curriculum" but also the lives of the parents, grandparents, and faculty as they live their lives before their children (2 Timothy 3:14-15).

As one reads the Epistles or letters that Paul sent to his students, one gains insight into the profile of an incarnational teacher.

Teachers (Models) should:

- *"...walk in a manner worthy of the calling with which you have been called" (Ephesians 4:1).*
- *Have renewed minds that are characterized by humility and sound-judgment (Romans 12:3, 16).*
- *Exercise their gifts (Romans 12:7-8).*

- *Love without hypocrisy, demonstrate empathy and be devoted to and honor one another (Romans 12:10).*
- *Evidence diligence and perseverance during hard times (Romans 12:11-12).*
- *Show empathy and practice hospitality by inviting students into fellowship (Romans 12: 13, 15).*
- *Respect what is right and never repay evil with evil (Romans 12:17).*
- *Be characterized as gentle, patient, tolerant (Ephesians. 4:2).*
- *Put aside anger and abusive speech (Colossians. 3:8).*
- *Show compassion and kindness (Colossians 3:12).*
- *Allow the peace and Word of Christ to dwell and rule in their hearts (Colossians 3:15-16).*

The Importance of Community

Spiritual formation happens within the context of community; therefore, life within the classroom is another element of the living curriculum. Classroom climate may be a second factor, but it too is controlled by the temperament, behavior and instructional practices of the teacher.

There will be times, on the occasional down day, when the classroom climate may feel a bit chilly, but when an uncomfortable coldness becomes the normal temperature, the climate may negate the message of the gospel. Program directors must be responsible for reading and controlling the climate, and, if needed, modify the temperature.

The epistles reveal Paul's interactions with his students and provide insight into Paul's other-directed values and relationships. Paul referred to Silvanus, Timothy and himself as being gentle among the Thessalonians and compared their care to that of "a nursing mother tenderly caring for her own children."

He also referred to their having a "fond affection" and finding pleasure in not only imparting the gospel of God but their own lives on their behalf. Paul, Silvanus and Timothy also had the hearts of a father as evidenced by how they exhorted, encouraged and implored each of them as a father would his children (1 Thessalonians 2: 7-11).

Paul prayed for and encouraged his "classroom" of new believers. He told them that he thanked God for them, that he longed to see them and assured them that he always remembered them in his prayers (Romans 1:8-11 and Philippians 1:2-4).

His prayers for them were joyful because they participated in the gospel together, and he envisioned God perfecting them in Christ and enabling them to abound in love and be filled with the fruit of righteousness (Philippians 1:6-11).

One can easily imagine the impact of being told by Paul that they were his hope, joy, glory, and crown of exultation (1 Thessalonians 2: 19-20).

Transformational classrooms are places where:

- The Holy Spirit empowers teachers to reflect the fruit of the Spirit
- Children are unconditionally loved and accepted
- Relationships are warm as opposed to cold or merely task oriented
- Children experience developmentally appropriate instruction and where varying levels of readiness are accommodated
- Trust abounds, and children feel safe
- All children think that they belong through opportunities to use their gifts and experience success.
- Children regularly laugh, play, work and share with one another
- Children are well-managed and biblical principles of discipline are exercised.
- Relationships are infused with grace
- Students are introduced to Shalom---the way things, in Christ, can and should be.

The Ongoing Battle

Christian school educators are on a mission to accomplish not only readiness for school but readiness for a life in Christ. In light of the weightiness of this responsibility, you may find yourself saying, "I can't. I am not able!" This, however, is an important confession in that it is at this point where Jesus says, "But I can."

THE CHRISTIAN LIFE AND THE LIFE OF AN INCARNATIONAL TEACHER REFLECTS OUR DEPENDENCE UPON THE SPIRIT OF GOD AND THE BODY OF CHRIST, NOT OUR INDEPENDENCE.

John Ortberg, in, *Everybody's Normal Till You Get to Know Them*, discusses an obstacle to creating community. Even though we were created for relationships, our flesh makes maintaining community difficult.[60]

When you deal with human beings, you have come to the "as is" corner of the universe. ...One of the great marks of maturity is to accept the fact that everybody comes "as is" ...Of course, the most painful part of this is realizing that I am in the "as is" department as well.

Every one of us pretends to be healthier and kinder than we really are, we all engage in what might be called "depravity management"... Every one of us---all we like sheep--- has habits we can't control, past deeds we can't undo, flaws we can't correct. This is the cast of characters God has to work with (pp. 14-17).

"All we like sheep" describes all the members of the Christian school--- administration, teachers, parents, and the children. If community is to be created and life in Christ modeled, then it must begin with admitting that one cannot do this on one's own.

Everyone within an early education program must acknowledge and deal with the "as is" flaw. Paul, once again, serves as a model.

He openly acknowledged that he struggled with his weaknesses.

He too struggled with sin and inconsistency.

He too was flawed.

He speaks of this in Romans 7 when he writes;

> *"For we know that the law is spiritual—but I am unspiritual, sold into slavery to sin. For I don't understand what I am doing. For I do not do what I want—instead, I do what I hate. But if I do what I don't want, I agree that the law is good. But now it is no longer me doing it, but sin that lives in me. For I know that nothing good lives in me, that is, in my flesh. For I want to do the good, but I cannot do it. For I do not do the good I want, but I do the very evil I do not want! Now if I do what I do not want, it is no longer me doing it but sin that lives in me.*
>
> *So, I find the law that when I want to do good, evil is present with me. For I delight in the law of God in my inner being. But I see a different law in my members waging war against the law of my mind and making me captive to the law of sin that is in my members. Wretched man that I am! Who will rescue me from this body of death?"*

> *Romans 7: 14-24, ESV*

Paul also testified to the solution.

He chose to live under the power of the Holy Spirit because he accepted the fact that in the flesh he couldn't, but in the Spirit, he could.

> *"For those who live according to the flesh have their outlook shaped by the things of the flesh, but those who live according to the Spirit have their outlook shaped by the things of the Spirit. For the outlook of the flesh is death, but the outlook of the Spirit is life and peace, because the outlook of the flesh is hostile to God, for it does not submit to the law of God, nor is it able to do so. Those who are in the flesh cannot please God.*

> ***You, however, are not in the flesh but in the Spirit***, *if indeed the Spirit of God lives in you. Now if anyone does not have the Spirit of Christ, this person does not belong to him. But if Christ is in you, your body is dead because of sin, but the Spirit is your life because of righteousness. Moreover, if the Spirit of the one who raised Jesus from the dead lives in you, the one who raised Christ from the dead will also make your mortal bodies alive through his Spirit who lives in you."*

> *Romans 8:5-1, ESV*

You have heard it said that those who do not acknowledge warfare will lose the battle.

THE ENEMY OF OUR FAITH IS NOT ON THE SIDE-LINE ROOTING FOR OUR SUCCESS WITHIN THE CLASSROOM.

The devil will actively work to draw attention away from the truth, tempt teachers and students to yield to the desires of the flesh, lie to us about who we are and our worth as individuals, and bring about divisions within our programs.

We must, therefore, hear Paul's exhortation to "put on the full armour of God so that you will be able to stand firm against the schemes of the devil" (Ephesians 6: 11). Paul goes on to say that "with all prayer and petition pray at all times in the Spirit" (v.19). He prayed for perseverance, boldness and that he might speak as he ought in making known the gospel (v. 20).

Paul acted upon the truth and not his feelings.

He acknowledged the fact that he couldn't and as a result became dependent on the Spirit and prayer. He knew that those he discipled, in their own strength, would likewise be unable and so he prayed that his students would be "rooted and established "in the love of Christ and that the Spirit would strengthen and empower them. (Ephesians 3:14-18, ESV)

TRANSFORMATIONAL TEACHERS ACCEPT THE RESPONSIBILITY TO DIE TO SELF AND BECOME MORE AND MORE LIKE CHRIST.

Dr. Robertson McQuilken, former president of Columbia International University, shared a straightforward formula for realizing a victorious life. The first step is the acknowledgment and confession of specific sins.

Confession must then be followed by "targeted" prayer and petition for the strength needed to stand firm and not give in to temptation. During this warfare, one should focus on meditating and memorizing related truths from God's word, and finally, invite another staff person to join them in warfare, share in their struggle and hold them accountable.[61]

Extending Knowledge and Beliefs into Practice

- Regularly study and encourage one another in the spiritual disciplines related to dependence on Christ and "walking in the spirit."
- Pray for and embrace the fruit of the Spirit
- Practice child directed as opposed to curriculum directed instruction. Know the children across all strands of their development and align practices with readiness as a means of limiting stress and experiencing success. View students as individuals.
- Demonstrate enthusiasm throughout your interactions
- Voice love and concern for your students
- Pray for each child and his or her families
- Claim your classroom, through a prayer walk around the room, for Christ and His work each day

Reflect and Respond

1. Stand back and frame the climate within your classroom or the classrooms within your program. Identify the climate that characterizes your classroom community. Is the community warm or cold in nature? What steps can be taken to represent Shalom better?

2. Compare your dispositions to those of an incarnational teacher. Are you able to invite your students to imitate you? Journal your conclusion.

3. Identify and confess areas of personal weakness or inconsistency. Are you willing to change and walk in a new direction? If so, what steps will you take?

4. When you fall short, and at times you will, what is your response to the students? Can you recall times when you confessed behaviors that were out of alignment with the reflection of Christ in your classroom?

5. Have you expanded your community to include the parents? What characterizes your relationship with parents? How often do you talk to them? What is the nature of your communication? Do you welcome them or try to avoid them?

6. Having walked through the process of laying the foundation for a Christian worldview, you no doubt sense the similarity of means across the chapters. This is because the means can and should be integrated. Just as a worldview is an integrated whole, so too are the means for developing a child's faith. The means are not independent instructional elements, but rather, when integrated, the whole of the child's experiences during the early childhood years. The next time someone asks you what curriculum you use what will be your answer?

Chapter Nine: Developing a Plan to Assess the Spiritual Growth of Young Children

...and He will put the sheep on His right and the goats on the left. Then the King will say to those on His right, 'Come, you who are blessed of My Father, inherit the kingdom prepared for you from the foundation of the world. 'For I was hungry, and you gave Me something to eat; I was thirsty, and you gave Me something to drink; I was a stranger, and you invited Me in; naked, and you clothed Me; I was sick, and you visited me; I was in prison and you came to Me...'Truly I say to you, to the extent that you did it to one of these brothers of Mine, even the least of these you did it to Me.'

Matthew 25: 33-34, 40 NASB

Now I exhort you, brethren, by the name of our Lord Jesus Christ, that you all agree and that there be no divisions among you, but that you be made complete in the same mind and in the same judgment. <u>For I have been informed concerning you,</u> my brethren, by Chloe's people, that there are quarrels among you.

1 Corinthians 1:10-11 NASB

Regularly evaluate early childhood programs in light of program goals, using varied, appropriate, conceptually and technically sound evidence to determine the extent to which programs meet the expected standards of quality and to examine intended as well as unintended results.

NAEYC and NAECS/SDE Position Statement[62]

The Need for a Plan

The element often neglected in discussions related to curriculum is the need for an assessment plan that verifies the effectiveness of the curriculum. We began this book on the distinctives of a Christian early education program with the need for a curriculum framework.

The framework clarifies a program's mission, vision, and outcomes. Once the outcomes are aligned with instructional means, a plan that identifies how each outcome will be assessed will need to be developed.

The need to validate is a matter of integrity.

All stakeholders, parents in particular, have not only a desire but a right to know whether or not the school is doing and accomplishing what it has been designed to do.

The appropriateness of assessing spiritual formation, or any affective standard, is questioned by some because they are a matter of the heart, and these matters are thus viewed as difficult or even impossible to assess. Nevertheless, it is possible to examine the words and actions that proceed from the heart.

JESUS FOCUSED ON THE HEART AS A MEANS OF DIFFERENTIATING HIS TEACHING "IN A WAY THAT CONNECTED TO THE HEARTS OF THE PEOPLE."[63]

There is also specific scriptural evidence of assessments related to spiritual matters. The chapter's introductory scriptures are examples of assessments that provided a basis for judgment.

Even though only God can fully know the heart, program or curriculum directors and teachers are nevertheless responsible for collecting and evaluating the data needed to judge whether or not the curriculum's content and strategies are resulting in the intended outcomes and, when needed, adjust the curriculum.

The Matthew twenty-five example of unobtrusive observation, found within Jesus' teaching on judgment, might be considered a checklist or the criteria that separated the sheep from the goats. The assessment was unobtrusive in that the subjects were unaware of the assessment and that what was done for "the least of these" was an indicator of their care for Jesus Himself.

The checklist identified behaviors that, from the viewpoint of the assessor, aligned with an individual's love for the Savior. Not only were the observations considered valid indicators but, in the case of early childhood, the method would be more reliable because the subjects were unaware they were being observed.

The example found within Paul's letter to the Corinthians (1:10-11) was in response to anecdotal information. Information or feedback had come to Paul that teaching had not yet changed or set apart the new believers from that of their Corinthian neighbors.

The information provided Paul with input not only that they needed more teaching in the area of being of one mind, but it provided a focus for content that still needed to be emphasized or retaught. Content within 1 Corinthians is responsive to that need.

Not only had he received an assessment, but he responded to it because the data gave evidence that his mission, "every man complete in Christ," had not yet been realized.

Early Childhood Assessment Standards

Before discussing the specifics of how spiritual formation goals might be assessed, principles of assessment related to early childhood must be understood and followed to assure that data is reliable or is an accurate snapshot of whether or not the children have reached or are moving toward the desired outcome. The reliability of data is measured by comparing the results of repeated assessments.

To what degree is the performance of the student consistent? Because the children during early childhood are immature, their performances may vary in that many variables can influence a child's performance on any given day.

THIS IS THE REASON THAT UNOBTRUSIVE OBSERVATIONS OVER TIME ARE A MEANS TOWARD GREATER RELIABILITY. A CHILD'S PERFORMANCE DURING DIRECT-OBSERVATION OR QUESTIONING DURING AN INTERVIEW WITH A TEACHER ARE DIFFERENT FROM A PERFORMANCE DURING A MORE CASUAL OBSERVATION.

Even something as simple as the answer to a recall question from a story can differ when responding directly or through the voice of a hand-held puppet because attention has shifted to the puppet and stress is thus reduced. Another factor related directly to reliability is whether or not the desired response to an assessment is something the child is used to doing.

TO ASK A CHILD TO SPEAK THROUGH A PUPPET TO SUMMARIZE A STORY IS ONLY RELIABLE IF THE CHILD IS FAMILIAR WITH USING A PUPPET WHEN ANSWERING QUESTIONS.

Because a single prompt or one assessment begs the question of whether or not the performance is reliable and given the fact that perfect reliability is not possible, assessors should use multiple indicators upon which to measure a given outcome.

Assessments must also be valid. It is valid only to the degree that reliable data is an indicator of the outcome being assessed. When measuring, for example, whether or not a child is demonstrating gratitude or thankfulness through an observational checklist, the performance and decision are only valid indicators if the criteria on the checklist align with behaviors related to the disposition in question (in this case gratitude).

A teacher, for example, may see a child sharing with another child, but that would not be a valid indicator of gratitude. A valid checklist will have behaviors that are accepted or based upon researched indicators of the trait. The indicators must likewise align with behaviors that were taught when learning what grateful children do and don't do.

In addition to being both reliable and valid, assessments must also be age appropriate, tied to a child's daily activities, performed by individuals that are familiar to the children and trained in using the assessment, collected through multiple sources, and then used purposefully.[64]

PURPOSEFUL ASSESSMENTS SHOULD FIRST AND FOREMOST BE ON BEHALF OF THE CHILDREN. THE DATA ALLOWS THE TEACHER TO ASSESS THE GROWTH OF CHILDREN AND THEREBY IMPROVE LEARNING BY PROVIDING GREATER DIFFERENTIATION.

The data also provides the insight needed to target curriculum revisions. Summative assessments, those given as children complete the program, are not to give a grade or make decisions like student retention.

These assessments are "grading" the curriculum in that the data reflects instructional effectiveness. Evaluating the curriculum is purposeful in that it will directly impact future learning. Curriculum effectiveness would be based upon the percentage of children, program completers, that satisfy the criteria of a given outcome.

The means through which young children are assessed must be developmentally appropriate. Appropriate methods include observations, a portfolio of work samples, checklists, anecdotal notations of participation and behavior, parent interviews and questionnaires, and teacher-student interviews.

IT SHOULD BE NOTED THAT A STANDARDIZED TEST IS NOT ON THE LIST.

Taking a standardized test involves variables that impact reliability (following directions, fine motor control, visual discrimination, test anxiety, etc.). When selecting or designing an assessment, the most reliable and valid option should always be the one chosen.

Designing the Plan

Early education programs, using the principles of appropriate assessment and the program's desired outcomes, should organize the strategies into an assessment plan. This plan outlines how each of the program's major outcomes will be assessed. The table below is an example of the data that should be included within a plan:

The Outcome	Type of Assessment	Criteria for Checklists and Performance Rubrics or Questions for Interviews and Questionnaires	Who will be responsible for preparing and administering the assessment? When will the assessment take place?	How will the data be aggregated and used? What statistic will determine success?

Let's return to the example of the relationship between an outcome and curriculum in chapter two (see page 8). The process of designing an assessment plan, through a series of questions, can also be applied to assessment.

The example below is based on assessing children at the end of kindergarten.

What is the outcome?

- Children will communicate with God beyond the use of memorized prayers

What might serve as valid indicators of success?

Are the indicators the answer to a question, the demonstration of a skill, or observed behaviors?

Children pray using their own vocabulary

The content of prayer varies and is not repetitious, i.e. prayers do not always start with "thank you for the day" or "God bless mommy and daddy."   These things are indicators that the child prays, but not indicators that they pray beyond memorized prayers as stated in the outcome.

- Is there an assessment already in place or does an existing assessment, through a minor adjustment like the addition of a question, facilitate its use?

  Student participation in prayer may have been noted in an on-going anecdotal record, while information on the nature of these prayers was not included and is therefore needed.

- If a new or additional assessment is needed, then what means will be both useful and practical?

  Even though the current assessment can be modified to accommodate the performance criteria, a second assessment would provide additional evidence. It might also be helpful to view it from a different angle.

The additional data might be available through a question during a parent conference or on an exit questionnaire. The question: Tell me about your child's prayers. Can you give me an example?

Note: This question would only follow the parent's affirmation that their child prays or prays more often. The child may have begun to pray more or volunteer to pray (a different outcome) but may not have begun to also pray in a conversational or personal way.

- Will the demonstration need a rubric or checklist to ensure objectivity?

  The answer is related to whether or not objectivity is needed. In this example, the affirmation that the child prays using his own vs. memorized words may be enough evidence of the outcome. However, if an example of the child's prayer is asked for or if there is the need for more specific criteria then either a checklist or rubric may be needed. The target performance, within a rubric, might involve the prayer not being memorized, in the child's language, or related to a specific need or activity, etc.

- At what point will the assessment be administered?

  Throughout the last semester (anecdotal record) before exiting the program and during the final parent conference or within the parent's exit questionnaire.

- Who will perform the assessment?

  This is simply a practical question but, once determined, assigns responsibility.

- How will the performance be changed into a number (measurement)? How will individual numbers be aggregated?

  If the performance related to a question is as simple as they can or cannot, then the total number in each category is all that is needed to aggregate the data and determine the percentage of children that have reached the desired outcome. In cases where a rubric is used to measure degrees of success, the number of children at each performance level would also serve as a measure.

  Rubrics clarify or provide objectivity by listing criteria for varying levels of a performance---target, acceptable, somewhat, or absent.

  The target performance in this example might be described as a prayer with content that is relevant to the child's current need or recent experience, expressed in their own words and offered voluntarily. The acceptable level would include two of the three criteria while the somewhat level only one.

  A value, based upon a three-point scale, can be assigned to each student 's performance so that the data can then be averaged as a means of determining the average performance of the group.

- What is the benchmark that must be met to verify the outcome? What is the percentage of students or program completers that satisfied the performance criteria?

  The benchmark (target percentage) relates to the group data. Many variables impact a student's performance; so, expectations need to be determined based upon these factors. In this example, a variable might be the numbers of children within the classroom that are from families where prayer is regularly practiced at home as opposed to the number of children from homes with no modeling of prayer. The expectation for the percentage of children reaching the desired outcome might be higher within a classroom where the majority of children are from Christian homes.

The variable is that the classroom is not the sole influencer and parent modeling would have been an additional instructional factor. In this example, the benchmark or success indicator might be 80%, while the expectation in classrooms where 75 % of the children are from unchurched homes the expectation might be as low as 40 to 45%.

The percentage is an arbitrary number and often at the discretion of a board or other form of governance.

Once the means of assessment for each outcome has been determined, the plan can then be summarized. The following plan, for example, might be applied at the end of kindergarten.

The Outcome	Type of Assessment	Criteria for checklists and performance rubrics or questions for interviews and questionnaires	Who will be responsible for preparing and administering the assessment? When will the assessment take place?	How will the data be aggregated and used? What statistic will determine success?
Skill Children will communicate with God beyond the use of memorized prayers.	Anecdotal Record Parent Interview	Evidence of prayers that are: Offered in the child's language Varied in content and then related to the needs or recent experiences of the child.	During the final quarter of Kindergarten by the child's teacher.	The number students who do and do not meet the criteria; presented as percentages with a benchmark of 75%.
Additional Examples				
Knowledge/Skill Children can offer a simple explanation of the Gospel.	Interview with a wordless book prompt (assuming the prompt is familiar to the children).	A checklist of keywords for each part of the explanation. Keywords: Sin, disobey, punishment, Jesus, cross, love, blood, forgive, pray, confess, believe, follow, heaven, eternal life.	A teaching assistant that the children know and who has been trained in the use of the checklist.	Percentage of children reaching the target and acceptable level of performance. Target: use of 9 key words with at least one rom each truth or "page" within the wordless book. Acceptable: 6 or 7 key words 85% of the group is at or above the acceptable level
Disposition Children care for and serve others	Observational Checklist	A running record checklist of verbs or actions that have been used and reviewed when discussing what children do and do not do when they care for someone or something.	Throughout the kindergarten year teachers and assistants will note the date when a child evidences care or service to others.	The total number of entries for each student. The percentage of the class that were at or above a benchmark number set at the beginning of the year

Extending Knowledge and Beliefs into Practice

Instruction should not only focus on appropriate means by which outcomes will be reached but also the performances that will verify the outcomes. For example, if children are to provide a simple explanation of the gospel, and vocabulary will be the basis of the assessment, then that vocabulary should align with the explanations used when introducing and teaching the gospel.

Even though a complete assessment plan may be written, the implementation of the plan should be gradual. Plan to start with a limited number of assessments and gradually add no more than two or three each year until the plan is completely implemented.

When developing a plan start with assessments that occur at one time like an interview. In the second year add an assessment that happens over time like the use of an on-going checklist. This will allow for assessors to have a single set of new behaviors to look for and record. If teachers, during the initial stages, must observe too many new things at once, the task can be overwhelming and the results unreliable.

UPON COMPLETING AN ASSESSMENT CONSIDER NOT ONLY THE DATA BUT THE ASSESSMENT ITSELF. DOES IT WORK? DOES IT NEED TO BE MODIFIED BEFORE THE NEXT USE?

Directors are responsible for providing an annual "State of the Mission" report. This report, outlining whether or not each outcome was satisfied, should be made available to all stakeholders ---the board, the faculty and staff of the program and the parents.

Faculty, under the direction of the program director, should focus on areas where performance falls below expectations.

For each area of concern address questions like:

- Was instruction implemented as planned?

- What modifications are needed? Should more time or emphasis be placed on this outcome?

- Is there a different instructional strategy or experience that might be more effective?

- Can the observed weakness be related to a unique variable that was present, i.e. a group of students that as a whole were developmentally younger and less ready?

- Is focused professional development needed?

Reflect and Respond

1. To what degree is your teaching characterized by "backward design"? Are you intentional about aligning your instruction with specific outcomes?

2. Are you currently using teacher conferences as a means of gaining insight into how the child is changing and growing? Are you taking time to record or journal evidence of student learning at the end of each parent conference? Who is doing the talking during a conference? Are you asking questions that are aligned with the desired outcomes of your program?

3. Can you identify changes in your program that were data driven? If not driven by data then what was the driving rationale for the change? For example, was it emotion, personal needs or another outside influence as opposed to student learning and the effectiveness of the curriculum?

Afterward

As I reflect upon what I have written, I realize again how fortunate and blessed I was to have been shown God's calling and vocational path early in life. Truly God *"satisfied me* in the morning with *His* loving kindness that I might sing for joy and be glad all *my* days"

Psalm 90:14

The Japanese have a concept, ***Ikigai***, that when translated means "a reason for being." This idea reflects the biblical perspective that God has designed each of us for a purpose. Even though this search, for some, may take many years and involve false starts, for some it is discovered during childhood. "Behaviors that make one feel ikigai are not actions one is forced to take---these are natural and spontaneous actions."[66] Christians believe that these actions are not by chance but created and designed by God. They are Spirit-prompted and directed.

Ikigai is seen as the intersection of several important dimensions that give meaning to life. Within it are elements that hopefully characterize Christian school educators, and you, the reader in particular.

There is no question that the world needs teachers committed to the education of young children. These children need an understanding of the reality of God, and that truth has been revealed to them in Scripture. Christian teachers embrace the advancing of God's kingdom among the children as mission (Matthew 28:19-20) and live it both personally and vocationally. Great teachers love children, what they teach and the mission that drives their labor. They view themselves as professionals, and thus, participate in ongoing opportunities to both grow in their understanding of children and the means through which their effectiveness can be maximized. Finally, the dividends are paid both through one's salary and throughout eternity.

My desire for you is that you view early childhood education and your role within it as a means of glorifying God and experiencing a life worth living. I also pray that, if not, that for the children's sake you will ask God to provide a renewed passion and or redirection so that you too can know and live in **"Ikigai."**

Appendix A

Spiritual Formation of the Young Child: A Checklist

Environment

- o Warm and inviting

- o Emotionally safe, well managed with minimal stress

- o A learning community as opposed to a classroom

- o Visual displays of God's Word and Values

- o Disciplined (authoritative) and orderly

- o Celebrates the uniqueness of each child and is culturally responsive

Faculty

- o Child-directed or directed in attitude and practice

- o Understand child development (cognitive, social, emotional, physical, spiritual)

- o Warm, loving, open and inviting

- o Behaviors and speech exemplify the fruit of the Spirit (models of growing relationship with Christ and a transformed life)

- o Teach with enthusiasm

- o Speak often of God and the things He is doing in their lives

- o Model biblical relationships, a teacher with a teacher, teacher with an administration, teacher with parents o Prayer for students and engage in spiritual warfare (stand against the enemy and claim their classrooms for Kingdom purposes)

Bible Teaching

o Focused on doing (prayer, worship, helping, etc.)

o Utilizes celebrations and focuses on holidays as teaching tools

o Taught through all the senses

o Leads to an appropriate response (obedience)

o Basic worldview questions are integrated into instruction and conversations:

- God / Jesus Created, Jesus Loves, God Provides (reality)

- God also made heaven. It is a wonderful place where Jesus' followers will someday live with Him

- The Bible is filled with God's words and will for us. What He says is true (Truth)

- There is a right and wrong. God defines, in His book, what is right and wrong. God tells us what is of value and what is beautiful (Value)

- God made us in His image. We are His special creation. He made us because He wants a relationship with us (Man)

- Man sinned and broke the relationship (The Problem)

- Jesus died to restore relationship etc. (Redemption, answer to the problem)

- Jesus is coming again to receive us and establish His kingdom (The future hope)

Content in alignment with spiritual development needs:

o Focus on stories that demonstrate God's care, concern, and trustworthiness toward those who trust in Him. "God is good. He loves and cares for you."

o Reflect the character of Christ (love, care, unconditional acceptance, warmth, giving, forgiveness, empathy) as a means of loving an unseen God.

o Stories that focus on obedience:

o Through <u>modeling</u> and stories, the children's picture of God is formed in their minds. Through understanding God's holiness and love, the stage is set to become His child through faith in Jesus

o Stories of self-sacrifice, submission, and selflessness become meaningful as they participate in acts of kindness toward others. God exemplified this through the giving of His Son (Matthew 25:31-37).

o Chapels geared to the nature and needs of the young child (active, shorter, etc.)

o Frequent opportunities to respond to the gospel (salvation) message

o Integrates children's literature into Bible instruction as a means of bridging to their lives

o Provides meaningful developmentally appropriate Bible memory (content, length, vocabulary)

o Forms basis for character integration across the curriculum

Academics

- Developmentally appropriate practices, content, and expectations

- Centered on new experiences, interactive language, activity, and play

- A balance between the affective and cognitive

- Integrate motor activities as critical to cognitive development (30% of daily schedule)

- Social development promoted through success and interactive learning

- God-centered teaching of general revelation

- Focus on clearly defined, integrated outcomes

Families

- Encouraged to participate

- Seen as a critical success factor

- Regularly involved in the school and classroom

- Provided with resources and instruction to assist them in their parenting roles

- Hold the same core spiritual values as the school or participate in parent education opportunities to bring about like-mindedness

- Are interviewed or surveyed as a means of assessing the spiritual growth of children during the early years

Elements for Unobtrusive Observation of the Children (Assessment)

- o Children:

  - Evidence enthusiasm during worship, prayer, Bible class

  - Pray in class and at home

  - Are developing a language for their faith

  - Provide basic answers to worldview questions
  - Care for one another

  - Appear confident and content

  - Are actively engaged in learning

  - Are respectful and obedient

  - Enjoy school

Appendix B

God's Redemptive Story

This annotated Big Story timeline was referenced in chapter seven. Even though you may be using Bible stories as the foundation for your curriculum, they should be presented, whenever possible, within the context of God's bigger redemptive story.

I also referred to *The Biggest Story* as an example or model for sharing the story. Become familiar with this version and then retell it in your own words, using language appropriate to the age and backgrounds of your students. When presenting a Bible story to the children you might use a phrase like, "Remember how people always wanted to do things their way instead of God's way? Today's story tells us about one of those times."

TBS: The Biggest Story: Keven DeYoung. Crossway. 2015. Also available in a DVD movie format and an ABC board book for children ages one to three.

In chapter six there was a reference to Rick Warren's book, *God's Big Plans for Me.* This book can identify opportunities to teach the children how God wants them to live and that God has a plan or purpose for their lives. When possible integrate these stories or use the applications related to God's plan and purpose for the children as a means of integrating worldview.

GBP: God's Big Plans for Me: Rick Warren. Zonderkidz, 2017.

The following Bible Story Books for young children are referenced throughout the outline:

JSB: The Jesus Storybook Bible. Sally Lloyd-Jones. Zonderkidz
TBB: The Beginner's Bible: Catherine DeVries. Zondervan
TBS: The Biggest Story: Keven DeYoung. Crossway.
TPB: The Preschooler's Bible. Gilbert Beers. David C. Cook
GBP: God's Big Plans for Me: Storybook Bible: Rick Warren. Zonderkidz

The pages from these books, that align with each portion of the timeline, are identified for your convenience. Note that some sections have few or no stories at all. This does not mean that they have less importance or that you should not include a preference of your own. Keep in mind, however, that during early childhood the focus should be on key concepts or ideas. The details surrounding the divided kingdom and its kings, for example, may be beyond their understanding. If a Bible Storybook is not referenced in a section of the outline, it is because that book contained no story related to that portion of the outline.

Introduction:

God has given us the Bible to tell us a wonderful story about His love for you and me. The Bible is a big book because it is a really big story. The Bible is made up of smaller stories that all belong together. You may have heard many of these stories---stories about Adam and Eve, Father Abraham, Moses, King David, Jesus and his followers, and the apostle Paul. All people have been and are part of this amazing story of God's redeeming love, and everyone means that both you and I are part of the story as well.

JSB: 12-17

Creation and Man's Purpose:

Eternity Past

Even though the story has a beginning, God had no beginning, and He has no end. He has always been alive, and He will never die. He does not have a body like you and me; He is a spirit. He is good, pure, and almighty. He lives in heaven. God has a plan for this world and for you and me. We will learn about that plan as we follow it through the pages of the Bible.

Creation

Even though God had no beginning, all stories do. Once upon a time, at the beginning of time, God decided that he wanted to create a beautiful world. The very first thing it says in the Bible is that "in the beginning, God created the heavens and the earth." God made the universe, the planets, the earth and all of nature. He made animals and plants to live on the earth, and His most wonderful creation was people. The Bible says that people were **made in His image**. So, when we see people who love each other and are able to make new things we can see a little bit of what God is like.

JSB: 12-17
TBB: 9-17
TBS: Chapter 1
TPB: 10-19
GBP: 8-21

Need for Salvation

Fall of Man

God gave them a beautiful garden called Eden in which to live. God told them to care for nature, start a family, and spend time with Him. He did not force them to do these things even though He hoped they would. He wanted them to love Him because they wanted to. **They were able to obey or choose to disobey.** God told them there was one tree in the garden from which they were not to eat because if they did they would die.

Adam and Eve were happy in the garden, but one day Satan came in the form of a serpent, and he told Eve that God did not really mean what He said about dying if she ate the fruit. Eve listened, was tempted and then took a piece of fruit from the tree and ate it. She also gave some to Adam. They were now **guilty of disobeying God**. This was the **very first sin**, and because of sin, they could no longer enjoy a **close relationship with God**. **They turned away from God, but God still wanted a friendship with them.**

He came to the garden and looked for them. **He promised them that someday he would send a Savior who would "crush" Satan and beat the power of sin and death.**

JSB: 28-37
TBB: 18-25
TBS: Chapter 1
TPB: 20-23
GBP: 22-27

Sin Worsens

Adam and Eve had two sons, and their names were Cain and Abel. Like their parents, they had sinful hearts. **God gave them a way that their sins could be forgiven. If they killed an innocent lamb and offered it to God, God would forgive their sins. Instead of a lamb**, Cain chose to bring vegetables from his garden as his offering to God. **Abel did what God had said** and brought a lamb, and God was pleased with Abel's lamb and Abel's obedience.

- Over the years the number of people increased until there were many people on the earth.
- They too sinned, and God decided that He would start over again
- Noah and the Flood
- After the flood, the people did not pay attention to God and were quite proud
- The tower of Babel
- The beginning of many languages and as a result people spread apart (which is what God wanted them to do in the first place).

JSB: 38-55
TBB: 26-38
TBS: Chapter 2
TPB: 24-35
GBP: 28-35

Channel of Salvation

The Patriarchs

The people may have moved apart and created different countries (nations) but, these people **still did not obey God and follow Him.** God decided to choose one man to create a group of people that would follow Him and be an example to all the other people on the earth. They were to show others that there is one true God who cares for them and wants to live among them. It is time for Father Abraham to enter the story. God told Abraham that he should leave his country and that He would show him a new land in which to live. **God made a promise, called a covenant, to Abraham**. He promised Abraham that He would make Abraham's people (descendants) a great people and there would be as many descendants as there were stars in the heavens. God said that **through Abraham's family, all the people on earth would be blessed.**

- The birth of Isaac,
- Abraham's obedience
- God's provision of a ram for sacrifice in place of Isaac
- Esau and Jacob

JSB: 56-75
TBB: 39-70
TBS: Chapter 3
TPB: 36-63
GBP: 36-47

Joseph

- Jacob (Israel) and his twelve sons
- Joseph sold into slavery by his jealous brothers and taken to Egypt
- Joseph, the interpreter of dreams, found favor with the King
- The predicted famine and Joseph's leadership
- Joseph reunited with his family

Even though what Joseph's brothers had done was meant to be bad, God used it for good. God sent Joseph to Egypt to save not only the people there but also his people, the people that belonged to God's promise. **God used Joseph to show the people of Egypt and his family that He was the true God, a God that does what He says he will do**. Joseph's whole family moved to Egypt.

The Israelites, descendants or children of Abraham, became a nation of over a million people. This is exactly what God promised Abraham that he would do. Before Joseph's father died he blessed his son Judah. **One of Judah's descendants would be a King, and all nations would be blessed by him and obey him (Gen. 49:10).**

JSB: 76-83
TBB: 71-91
TPB: 64-75
GBP: 48-55

The Exodus from Egypt

- Moses
- The ten plagues
- Freedom to return to the land
- The Red Sea

During the last plague, the oldest son in every house died. God, however, provided a way for the sons of the Israelites to be saved. The family was to put the **blood of a lamb** on the doorpost of their house. When the angel of death saw the blood, the house would be passed over, and the oldest son would not die. God saved the those who did what God had said through the blood of a lamb. The people had a long hot trip across the desert in front of them. The trip was very hard. There was no food or water, and they even had to fight a battle against another enemy. **God, as always, was faithful and gave them water, manna, and quail for food, and victory in their battle.**

JSB: 84-99
TBB: 92-119

TBS: Chapter 4
TPB: 76-107
GBP: 56-75

The Law

- The Ten Commandments
- The golden calf
- God's judgment upon their idolatry

JSB: 100-107
TBB: 120-123
TBS: Chapter 5
TPB: 108-111

Wandering

After their long journey back to the land promised to Abraham, the people stopped in a place called Kadesh-Barnea. They wondered what they would find when they entered the land, so Moses sent twelve men to go and check it out. When they came back eight of the men were really afraid. They said that there were giants in the land and very large cities with walls built around them. Two of the men, **Joshua and Caleb**, were not afraid because they had faith that God would go with them and give them victory.

They believed God would do as He had promised and give them their land. The people complained and wished they were back in Egypt (imagine that). God was again angry with them **because of their lack of faith in Him and His power**. God made them stay in the desert for forty more years. None of that group was allowed to go into the land except for the **two men of faith**, Joshua and Caleb, and those born after what happened at Kadesh-Barnea.

TPB: 116-127

Conquest

The time finally came when the Israelites were ready to enter the land that was promised to them. Joshua was now their leader. While the Israelites camped across the Jordan River from the land, two spies were sent into the land. In Jericho, the men were helped by a lady who lived there. Her name was Rahab. She gave them a hiding place so they would be safe from the soldiers and told them that the people had heard of their God's mighty acts and that they were afraid of them.

The spies told her that they would make sure that **she and her family would be safe because she trusted them and their God.** After the city was conquered, Rahab joined the people of Israel and became one of them. **Even though she was not an Israelite and had a sinful past, her belief and trust in the God of Israel saved her.** And she even became one of Jesus' grandmothers.

JSB: 108-115
TBB: 124-135
TPB: 128-135

Land Divided

Once they conquered all the areas of the land called Canaan, it was time to divide up the land. You may remember that Jacob had twelve sons. Now each of those sons had many descendants, and all the Israelites knew which son they were related to. They grouped themselves together into tribes (Reuben, Simeon, Levi, Judah, Zebulun, Issachar, Dan, Gad, Asher, Naphtali, Manasseh, Ephraim, and Benjamin). Joshua gave each tribe a part of the promised land. The tribe of Levi had been assigned to be the priests who would serve God and assist the people in worshiping God at the tabernacle. So, instead of giving them one part of the land, they were given cities in each of the parts.

The Judges

The Israelites settled in their new land and, just like so many times before, they began to forget all that God had done for them in bringing them to Canaan. **They did not obey God's law**. For over 300 years the same thing happened over and over again. The people would sin by not doing what God had told them to do when they entered the land. They did not drive their enemies out of the land, they married the women who were not Israelites and worshiped their strange gods. God would again punish the Israelites through an enemy army. **The defeated people would cry out to God, repent, and ask God for his forgiveness by worshiping Him and bringing the proper sacrifice**. Because **God is gracious**, He would send them **a deliverer** who would lead them in another victory and back to worshiping God.

- Some of the deliverers were Samson, Deborah, and Gideon.
- Story of Ruth, another one of Jesus' grandmothers
- One of the deliverers, also referred to as a judge, was Samuel. He was raised in the house of God and was a priest, prophet, and leader. Other nations had kings as leaders. The Israelites saw this, and they too wanted a king. They asked Samuel to appoint a king. Even though God wanted to be their ruler, the people wanted a person to trust and lead them. They wanted to be like everyone else.

TBB: 136-155
TPB: 136-151
GBP: 82-87

The United Kingdom

Saul was the first king that Samuel anointed. The people were now a Kingdom. Like so many kings that would follow him, Saul was disobedient to God. He, for example, after defeating the Philistines, offered sacrifices himself instead of waiting for the priest as God had commanded. God had to punish his sin by not allowing one of his sons to be the next King. **Samuel chose David, the shepherd boy** who stood up against the giant that mocked God, to be the next king. **David, from the family of Judah,** continued to trust God and while he was king **God continued to keep his promise to Abraham** and the nation of Israel became great. David wrote many Psalms, songs of praise to God.   One of the Psalms sang about how Israel had been blessed to be a blessing to all the nations of the earth (Ps. 67).

God said David's throne would last "forever" and that He would send a Savior through his family line. David was not perfect. He was also a sinner, but **David repented of his sins, and God forgave him.**

- King Solomon

JSB: 116-135
TBB: 156-200
TBS: Chapter 6
TPB: 152-175
CBP: 88-99 and 106-109

The Divided Kingdom

NOTE: This section and the three that follow should be simplified as a time period when the Kingdom and its Kings continually fell back into sin.

 God provided prophets to warn the people of their sins and the consequences that would happen if they failed to repent. Most of the kings were evil and as might be expected the people again worshiped idols. God's patience ran out. He sent the Babylonians to destroy the temple and city of Jerusalem and take the people away from their land. Even though the nation was evil, **some people among them were faithful.**

There was always a faithful group to keep belief in God alive. **Shadrach, Meshach, Abednego, and Daniel were examples**. They, even when everyone was worshipping idols, worshipped God alone and were willing to die in the fiery furnace rather than deny the one true God. **God saved them because they trusted Him**. This showed the Babylonians that Daniel's God indeed was God Almighty.

JSB: 136-151
TBB: 201-239
TBS: Chapter 6

TPB: 176-199

The Northern Kingdom Conquered

JSB: 159-169
TBB: 247-265
TBS: Chapter 7

Judah Alone and the Babylonian Captivity

JSB: 152-158
TBB: 240-246
TBS: Chapter 7
TPB: 208-219
GPB: 110-115

Return of the Remnant

A new nation arrived and took over Babylon. After many years, the Medes and Persia's king, allowed 50,000 Jews to return to their homeland. Zerubbabel was their leader. Esther, an Israelite, had married the King and God used her to encourage the King to allow her people to leave. Once back in the promised land, they rebuild the city of Jerusalem and the temple. The priest, Ezra, took about 2000 more Jews back to Jerusalem eighty years later.   Ezra taught the Law of God to the people. Then Nehemiah also brought back another 6000 people to help rebuild the walls of Jerusalem. **A remnant (or a group) of Abraham's descendants were once again back in their promised land.**

JSB: 170-175
TPB: 200-203
GPB: 100-105

Preparation for Salvation

It is at this point that the history, as written in the Old Testament, stops being recorded. God was silent for 400 years, but God's promise to send a Savior to bless all the nations of the earth had not yet happened. **The Prophet Micah, for example, said that the Savior would be born in Bethlehem, but that had not yet happened. God had kept His other promises so surely God would keep this promise as well.** The people continued to be persecuted by the rulers, and they waited....

This is a good time in the story to pause and think about some of the important truths that God has revealed in this True Story.

- God made the heavens and the earth including you and me
- God wanted a relationship with his most special creation—people
- People wanted things their way and beginning with Adam and Eve, men and women have had a sinful heart
- God gave a way to be forgiven—the offering of a lamb
- God's people would forget Him and disobey him over and over again
- God chose a man, Abraham, to be the father of a blessed nation. He promised Abraham a land, and that one day one of his descendants would be their Savior
- The people did become a great nation, and the people of this nation again went their own way. Over and over God had to punish their disobedience, and they had to repent and bring a sacrifice over and over again. God, in spite of their behavior, remained faithful to them and His promise.
- There always were some people who remembered Him, worshiped Him and expected Him to do what he had promised
- Now God was waiting for the right time to send the promised Messiah, a Savior for not only Israel but all the people and nations on the earth.

Purchase of Salvation

Incarnation: The Long-Awaited Savior

JSB: 176-199
TBB: 266-307
TBS: Chapter 8
TPB: 220-243
BPB: 116-129

Jesus' Works and Words

JSB: 200-285
TBS: Chapter 8
TPB: 244-359
GPB: 130-176

The Crucifixion: The Final Sacrifice

JSB: 286-309
TBB: 442-452
TBS: Chapter 8
TPB: 360-371
GPB: 177-188

The Resurrection: Victory Over Death

JSB: 310-317
TBB: 453-464
TBS: Chapter 9
TPB: 372-275
GPB: 189-197

Ascension

One day, when Jesus was about to return to heaven, he told the disciples to go and make disciples of all nations by baptizing them and teaching them to obey everything Jesus had told them to do. He said that he would always be with them.

This command is called the **Great Commission**. If you are hearing this story today, it is because a follower of Jesus is doing what God has commanded. They are obeying the great commission. Jesus wanted all people to become part of His story. He wants you to be part of this story too.

JSB: 318-325
TBB: 466-472
TBS: Chapter 9
TPB: 376-379
GPB: 198-203

Proclamation of Salvation

The Holy Spirit and Acts of the Apostles

JSB: 326-333
TBB: 473-503
TBS: Chapter 9
TPB: 380-411
GBP: 198-203

Explanation of Salvation

The Epistles: Letters to the Churches

JSB: 334-341
TPB: 412-end
GBP: 208-219

Climax of Salvation

Revelation

In the book of Revelation, the last pages in the Bible, we are told parts of God's story that will happen in the future. Satan has been at work throughout the history of the world. Just as he tempted Adam and Eve to disobey God, he has been deceiving people all over the world. Since people are still born with sin in their hearts, wickedness will continue to increase on the earth. Finally, **Jesus will come back to the earth** as a conquering king and will defeat the armies of Satan. **Those who have not confessed their sins asked Jesus for forgiveness will be separated from God forever. Those who chose to believe in and follow Jesus will spend eternity in heaven with God and Jesus and all the faithful people who have put their trust in God and His son Jesus.**

GBP: 201-207

Eternity future

The Bible ends by describing what is happening in heaven now and what will continue through all time. John, a disciple of Jesus, was given a vision in which he saw a great crowd of people, so big no one could count them, **they were from every nation and group of people on the earth.** They were wearing white robes and were holding palm branches in their hands.

They were saying, in a very loud voice, "Salvation belongs to our God, who sits on the throne and to the Lamb." God is worthy of worship from all people. Remember that God had promised Abraham that all the peoples of the earth would be blessed through him and John's vision showed that this has and will be true.

Remember that as the story began, I told you that you and I are also part of the story. **We also have to make a choice about who we will worship and follow.**

God loves us and therefore wants us to be his friend and walk with Him. He does not want us to go our own way and be like those that chose to disobey Him.   We too are sinners, want to go our own way, and we too need forgiveness. **God has given us a choice. The Good News, called the Gospel, is that we can be forgiven through Jesus, the lamb of God, who died to pay for our sins. We can choose to be followers of Jesus and live with Him forever.**

JSB: 342-348
TBB: 504
TBS: Chapter 10
GPB: 220-223

Appendix C

A Holiday "Curriculum"

The Celebration	Theme	Biblical References
These celebrations are offered as examples and options. Programs should feel free to add or delete based on developmental appropriateness, school calendar, curriculum alignment, and other cultures etc.	Romans 14:5-8 Regardless of the celebration, celebrate as unto the Lord and for His glory	Not intended for Bible Memory but for the basis for the themes.
Labor Day	The importance of calling (designed for a special work) and Glorifying God through our work	2 Timothy: 1: 8b -9 Colossians 1:28-29
Grandparents Day Celebrated at different times around the world	Respect for elders, their love and wisdom	Proverbs: 4: 20-22
Halloween	The evening before the church "turned" from darkness into light, declaring the truth in a culture that does not know it	Acts 26:16-18
Thanksgiving	In all things give thanks	Psalm 100: 4-5
Christmas	From heaven to a stable for you and me	Luke 2:1-20

New Year's Day Chinese New Year is celebrated according to Lunar Calendar	God's faithfulness over the past year and anticipating His presence in the new year	Psalm 89:1-2
Martin Luther King's Birthday	All men created equal yet unique	Galatians 3:28 John 8:36 Acts 7:34
Valentine's Day	Abiding in and Sharing God's Great Love	John 15:9-11 1 Corinthians 13
Washington's Birthday	The importance of God's word as the foundation for a country	Deuteronomy 6:1-3
St. Patrick's Day	A Focus on Missions	Matthew 28:19-20
Pre-Easter 6 weeks	Christ's ministry of love	Selected Teaching and Events John 2-11
Easter	He Lives	John 20
Earth Day April 22	Stewardship of God's creation	Genesis 1:28-30
Mother's Day	Honor mothers and their importance to the family	Ephesians 6:2
Memorial Day	Christ calls on Christians to lay down their lives for Him and for the freedoms we enjoy	John 15:13
Flag Day	Respect for Country and its Leaders	Romans 13:1-4
Father's Day	Honor fathers and their importance to the family	Matthew 19:19
National Independence Day Celebrations	God has ordained and established nations and governments. Pray for our Country and its leaders.	Romans 13

Special Note: Add appropriate state or national holidays, where appropriate, that are unique to your country or that represent cultural diversity and a global perspective within your classroom.

Appendix D

Early Childhood Stages: Comparisons		
Piaget	**Kohlberg**	**Fowler**
Birth to Two **Sensorimotor Stage** Reality is based on sensory input. Children form mental representations (schema) of an object	**Infancy** **Obedience/Punishment** Choices are made based upon the avoidance of punishment	**Birth to Two** **Primal Faith** The child learns to trust through bonding experiences with parents or other primary care providers. Trust is learned within a nurturing environment where basic needs are consistently addressed (Erickson)
Early Childhood Years **(ages 2-7)** **Preoperational Stage** Children can think about reality symbolically. An object can represent or stand for something else, i.e., a block can represent a car during play. Thinking is often egocentric in that the viewpoint of others is not considered or understood.	**Pre-School and Early Elementary** **Self-Interest** Interest shifts to rewards as opposed to punishment. Child behaves according to what is perceived as his or her best interest.	**Preschool / Kindergarten** **Intuitive-Projective or Impressionistic** Fantasy and reality are often mixed together. Most basic understandings about God are learned through impressions/experiences within the family or other surroundings (lasting impressions)
Middle and Upper Elementary School **(ages 7-11)** **Concrete Operational** The child thinks through images or symbols that represent reality as opposed to needing to rely on first-hand objects or experiences. Understanding, though arrived at mentally, .is not yet based upon logical thought.	**School-age** **(middle and high school)** **Conformity and Interpersonal Accord Conformity** Choices are based upon seeking approval and belonging. This characterizes preteens and adolescents.	**School Age** **Mythic-Literal** Children begin to understand their world in a more logical way. They accept the stories told by their faith community and understand them more literally. It is at this stage that a faith narrative is learned.

Note: Many individuals do not move beyond the concrete operational stage	Note: Moral stages do not always vary according to age, i.e., a child that is beyond preschool or even an adult can still be motivated by the avoidance of punishment.	Note: Fowler's stages are faith stages that are viewed as applicable to all religious belief systems. It is not a stage theory based upon the development of Christian faith and does not consider the influence of the Holy Spirit

Distinctively Christian

Christ-centered Professional Development
for Early Childhood Educators

Book One - Early Childhood Spiritual Development

Book Two - Early Childhood Philosophy and Principles

Book Three - Early Childhood Teaching and Learning

Learn more at www.WheatonPress.com

References

---

[1] Moreland, J.P. *Love Your God with All Your Mind: The role of reason in the life of the soul.* Colorado Springs: Co. NavPress. 2012.

[2] Zais, Robert. *Curriculum: Principles and Foundation.* New York: Crowell 1976.

[3] Postman, Neil. *The End of Education.* New York: Alfred A. Knopf. 1995. Chapter 1. Postman discusses the proposition that, a school without a worthy focus or narrative, is a school where learning has no meaning and students have reason to learn.

[4] The diagram of the relationships within a curriculum framework and the process discussed within this chapter are an adaptation of notes within an unpublished notebook developed by Dr. Connie Michell and myself for use in a pre-conference workshop, "Assessment of Student Learning: Developing and Implementing a Conceptual Framework", The Association of Biblical Higher Education, February, 2010.

[5] This mission is based upon the curriculum framework created by the primary (Preschool – 2nd) faculty at Ben Lippen School, a ministry of Columbia International University, Columbia, SC.

[6] The vision of Ben Lippen School's primary (Pre-K through 2) unit.

[7] Bohlmann, Katherine. *Grandma, What is Prayer?* St. Louis: Concordia. 2002.

[8] Bonner, Susan. My Whole Self Before You: A Child's Prayer and Learning Guide Modeled after the Lord's Prayer. Traverse City, Michigan: Kid Niche Publisher. 2012.

[9] See Appendix D for a comparison of Piaget, Kohlberg and Fowler.

[10] Fowler, James. 1992. *Christian Perspectives on Faith Development.* Asltey, Jerff and Francis, Leslie editors. Herefordeshire: England. Gracewing Fowler Right Books and Grand Rapids, Michigan: Eerdmans Publishing. Chapter 1.

[11] Flowler, James.

[12] Flowler. James.

[13] Retrieved online on May 3, 2018. https://childdevelopmentinfo.com/child-development/erickson/#.WutWoqQvxOM

[14] Simms, Eva. *The Child in the World: Embodiment, Time and Language in Early Childhood.* Detroit: Wayne State University Press. 2008. Simms references David Elkind's use of the term frame to refer to the child's understanding of regularly occurring sequential events. Frames, for example, might include a bedtime, classroom calendar or evening meal routine.

[15] Howse, Brandon P. "National Test Reveals Christian Students Lack and Christian Worldview". Retrieved on May 15, 2018. http://k.b5z.net/i/u/2167316/f/Lecture_3_What_is_a_worldview_Bethel_Revised_1.pdf

[16] Barna, James, *Transforming Children into Spiritual Champions.* Grand Rapids: MI: Baker Books. 2003. Chapter 2.

[17] Fakkema, Mark. *Christian Philosophy and its Educational Implications.* Chicago: NACS. 1952. B.1.5

[18] Moore, Russell. "How Do You Explain the Trinity to Children. Retrieved online on November 16, 2018. https://www.russellmoore.com/2016/04/28/how-do-you-explain-the-trinity-to-children-2/

[19] Zuck, Roy B. and Clark, Robert E. editors. *Childhood Education in the Church.* Chicago: Moody. 1975,

---

[20] Katz. Lilian G. (2013) What is Basic for Young Children?, Childhood Education, 54:1, 1619, DOI: 10.1080/00094056.1977.10728352

[21] Retrieved on May 15, 2018: https://www.childrendesiringgod.org/documents/curriculum/scope/abc_expanded.pdf

[22] Garrick, Gene. *Introduction to Christian Philosophy Applied to the Christian School.* Norfolk, Va: Tabernacle Church of Norfolk. p.12

[23] Garrick, Gene. p.24

[24] Holmes, Arthur. *All Truth is God's Truth.* Grand Rapids, MI: Eerdmans Publishing Co.1977. *p.32*

[25] Garrick, Gene. p.28

[26] Retrieved on January 5, 2019. http://www.dltk-bible.com/poems-bible.htm

[27] Retrieved on May 2, 2018 from: https://www.dts.edu/departments/academic/eml/sf/definition

[28] Garrick, Gene. p.31

[29] Refer to Appendix D

[30] Retrieved on May 2, 2018, from https://www.psychologynoteshq.com/kohlbergstheory

[31] Damon, William, *The Moral Child: Nurturing Children's Natural Moral Growth.* New Youk: Free Press as is referenced in Uecker, Milton. *Foundations of Christian School Education.* Colorado Springs: Purposeful Design. 2003. P. 229

[32] Uecker, Milton. *Foundations of Christian School Education. Colorado Springs: Purposeful Design. 2003*

[33] Coles, Robert. *The Moral Intelligence of Children. New York:* Putnam. 1998. P.16.

[34] Foster James. Helen. Media Services Coordinatorl. San Diego County Office of Education. Retrieved online on May 15, 2018. https://ats.apsva.us/wp-content/uploads/legacy_assets/ats/e7c909cc71-character-traits-hfj.pdf

[35] Smith, Christian and Lundquist, Melina. 2005. The Religious and Spiritual Lives of American Teenagers. Oxford Press.

[36] Butler, J. Donald. *Four Philosophies and their Practice in Education and Religion.* Third edition. New York: Harper and Row. 1968. p. 558.

[37] Childs, John L. as referenced in Garrick page 13. The quote was taken from *Education and Morals, page 57.*

[38] Garrick, Gene p.15

[39] Garrick, Gene p.16

[40] Dr. Hatch's courses and lectures are available through the Hatch Library collection at Columbia International University

[41] Dweck, Carol. Ideas related to resiliency and "not yet" are the basis for the need to help children understand that when they can't it is not due to lack of ability but rather the realization that the ability is yet to come. An overview of Dr. Dweck's work can be accessed online. For an example see www.youtube.com. Watch?v=J-swZaKN21c

[42] Anderson, M and Johnson, T. 2013. *GIST: The Essence of Raising Life Ready Kids.*

[43] Warren, Rick. *God's Big Plans for Me: Storybook Bible.* Grand Rapids, MI: Zonderkidz. 2017. Stories are based on stories from Hurlbut's *The Complete Book of Bible Stories.* Edited by Jon Walker.

[44] Hays, Edward. In *Childhood Education in the Church*, Chicago: Moody. 1975. p.153 and 159

[45] Tripp, Ted. *Shepherding a Child's Heart.* Wapwallopen. Pa: Shepherd Press. 1995

[46] Postman, Neil. *The End of Education.* New York: Alfred A. Knopf. 1995

47 Goldstone, Lawrence and Nancy. *Deconstructing Penguins.* New York: Random House. 2005

48 Barna, James, *Transforming Children into Spiritual Champions.* Grand Rapids: MI: Baker Books. 2003. P.

49 Stetzer, Ed. "Making Sure Children Actually Hear the Gospel and Not Just a Bunch of Bible Stories." ChristianityToday. February 2015, Retrieved online, April 2018: https://www.christianitytoday.com/edstetzer/2015/february/making-sure-children-actually-hear-gospel-and-not-just-bunc.html

50 Special thanks to Christa Anderson Dysart, a graduate of CIU's teacher education program. Christa was not only a student in Norfolk Christian's lower school when I was principal, but also, a teacher education student at CIU.   All teacher education students at CIU take a "Teaching Bible" course in which they illustrate and write their version of the redemptive story for use within their classrooms. Christa graciously allowed me to use her narrative as the basis for the abbreviated appendix version. My modifications were made for use with younger children and as an example for readers. Teachers should adapt the language and length to fit their students better.

51 DeYoung, Kevin. *The Biggest Story.* Illustrated by Don Clark. Wheaton: Crossway. 2015. Discovering this book and its amazing illustrations during the writing of this book was a gift from God. The book is also available in a DVD version and is an equally valuable resource.

52 The Four Bible Story Books for young children: *The Jesus Storybook Bibl*e. Sally Lloyd-Jones. Zonderkidz. *The Beginner's Bible*. Catherine DeVries. Zondervan. *The Preschooler's Bible*. Gilbert Beers. David C. Cook. *God's Big Plans for Me*. Rick Warren. ZonderKidz.

53 Browne, Chris. *Beyond the Walls: Equipping Students to Leave school without leaving their faith. 2012. p.80*

54 Joy, Donald in Zuck and Clark editors. *Childhood Education in the Church.* Chicago: Moody. 1975. Chapter 1. p 19-20

55 Hayes, Edward in Zuck and Clark editors. Childhood Education in the Church. Chicago: Moody 1975. Chapter 11. p.159.

56 Spackman, Carl K. *Parents Passing on the Faith.* Victor Books: Scripture Press. 1989, p. 76.

57 Piper. John. 1980 Sunday evening message to congregation. Retrieved online on November 16. 2018 https://www.desiringgod.org/messages/the-children-the-church-and-the-chosen

58 Gaebelein, Frank. Retrieved on May 15, 2018. https://biblicalstudies.org.uk/pdf/grace-journal/03-3_27.pdf

59 Garrick, Gene. p. 55

60 Ortberg, John. *Everybody's Normal Until You Get To Know Them.* Grand Rapids, MI. Zondervan. 2014.

61 McQuilken, Robertson. Dr. McQuilken, former president of Columbia International University, has authored numerous articles and books dealing with Sanctification and the Victorious Life. The steps outlined here are based upon his writings and messages during CIU chapels.

62 Retrieved on March 14, 2018. A Joint Position Statement of the National Association for the Education of Young Children (NAEYC) and the National Association of Early Childhood Specialists in State Departments of Education (NAECS/SDE.

63 Browne, Chris. Beyond the Walls. p.79

---

[64] For additional assessment guidelines refer to NAEYC's statement on Curriculum, Assessment, and program evaluation.
[66] Retrieved online on April 10, 2018: Wikipedia. https://en.wikipedia.org/wiki/Ikigai

Information regarding the stages of cognitive, social, moral, and faith development are easily accessible through online searches.
Websites used in compiling these comparisons were retrieved on May 3, 2018:
http://www.psychologycharts.com/james-fowler-stages-of-faith.html
https://www.psychologynoteshq.com/kohlbergstheory/
https://www.simplypsychology.org/piaget.html#stages

www.EngagedSchools.com

Made in the USA
Columbia, SC
28 July 2019